ENTERTAINMENT TECHNOLOGY PRESS

In taking advantage of the latest in 'print on demand' digital printing techniques, Entertainment Technology Press is approaching book publishing in a very different way. By establishing a wide range of highly specific technical books that can be kept up-to-date in a continuing publishing process, our plan is to cover the entertainment technology sector with a wide range of individual titles.

As will be seen by examining the back cover of this book, the ETP list is divided into various categories so as to allow sufficient room for generic growth and development of each title. To ensure the quality of the books and the success of the project the publishers are building up a team of authors who are practising in and well-respected by the industry. As specialists within a particular field of activity it is anticipated that each author will stay closely involved with 'their' title or titles for an extended period.

All Entertainment Technology Press titles have a dedicated area on the publisher's own website at www.etnow.com where latest information and up-dates can be accessed by purchasers of the books concerned. This additional service is included within the purchase price of all titles.

Readers and prospective authors are invited to submit any ideas and comments they may have on the Entertainment Technology Press series to the Series Editor by email to editor@etnow.com.

D1465282

Th Studi   C   EG
Tel   30806

ALUMINIUM STRUCTURES IN THE ENTERTAINMENT INDUSTRY

Peter Hind

ENTERTAINMENT TECHNOLOGY PRESS

Application & Techniques Series

To my daughters
Rebecca, Catherine, Sophie and Megan

ALUMINIUM STRUCTURES IN THE ENTERTAINMENT INDUSTRY

Peter Hind

Entertainment Technology Press

Aluminium Structures in the Entertainment Industry

© Peter Hind

First publication May 2001

A title in continuous publication within the
Entertainment Technology Press Application & Techniques Series
Series editor: John Offord

Published by Entertainment Technology Press Ltd
The Studio, High Green, Great Shelford, Cambridge, CB2 5EG
Internet: www.etnow.com

ISBN 1 904031 06 4

ASEI / 005 - 01/04

ABOUT THE AUTHOR

Peter Hind was born in 1958 and was educated at Bolton School and King's College, University of London. He is a Chartered Engineer, a Member of the Institution of Civil Engineers and a Fellow of Institution of Structural Engineers, England.

After graduation in 1980, the early part of his career was spent in London working for a firm of consulting engineers. After qualifying in 1984, he became an associate and subsequently a partner in a firm of consulting engineers and was responsible for the structural engineering work for many European and World concert tours between 1984 and 1996.

He joined Total Fabrications Ltd in Birmingham, England in 1996 as Chief Engineer and was subsequently appointed Technical Director. Peter left the UK in early 2002 and was appointed VP Engineering at Total Structures, Inc in California, USA. He is responsible for the structural engineering design work within the group.

Peter is the author of a number of articles published in *Protocol* magazine, the quarterly journal of the Entertainment and Services Technology Association, New York, USA. He is a member of the Rigging Working Group of the Technical Standards Committee of ESTA responsible for writing the ANSI standard on the design, manufacture and use of truss and tower sections. He is heavily involved in the writing of an ANSI standard on Temporary Stage Roofs.

Peter was an active member of the Task Group rewriting *Temporary Demountable Structures* as published by the Institution of Structural Engineers, England in March 1999. He also contributed to *Guide to Health, Safety and Welfare at Pop Concerts and Similar Events* as published by Health and Safety Commission and BS 7905 and BS 7906 *Lifting Equipment for Performance, Broadcast and Similar Applications* for the British Standards Institute.

Peter was a member of the Council and the Engineering Practice Committee of the Institution of Structural Engineers, England between 2000 and 2002 and is currently a corresponding member of the Advisory Group on Temporary Structures (AGOTS).

CONTENTS

ACKNOWLEDGEMENTS

The encouragement and help from many people from various corners of the entertainment industry and beyond is gratefully acknowledged and much appreciated.

They include Alan Jacobi at Unusual Rigging Limited, Chris Cronin at Total Fabrications Limited, Ian Coles at Total Structures, Inc, Wally Blount at Columbus McKinnon Corporation, Karl Ruling, Technical Manager of ESTA and Lynn Kennedy, the editor of Protocol magazine.

Most of all, thank you to my wife, Pauline for her love, support and patience.

INTRODUCTION

The use of temporary and permanent structures in the entertainment industry has mushroomed over recent years. In the past, these structures tended to be modest affairs, erected without proper consultation with the statutory authorities or professional structural engineers.

Since I designed my first aluminium roof structure for the entertainment industry nearly 20 years ago, I have witnessed ever more complex structures being contemplated and used. Some large projects, whilst being of a temporary nature, should be seen as significant construction and engineering tasks involving a considerable number of people from a variety of disciplines.

I have contributed to a number of ground-breaking projects over the years and have been heavily involved with writing standards. It is with this in mind that a number of people have encouraged me to write a book about aluminium structures which are in everyday use in the entertainment industry throughout the world.

It is written to assist a number of different groups of people:

Riggers - practical applications, positioning and support of equipment
safely, design parameters of truss.

Owners - thorough inspection, points to consider.

Users - basic inspection techniques, choosing correct truss, load
capacity, response to load.

Engineers - those interested in technical aspects.

*Those considering purchasing or hiring structures for use in
the entertainment industry* - insight into complexities.

In order to use the equipment safely in the entertainment industry, it is necessary to understand something about structures and materials, how trusses are designed, ground support, wind loading, stages, operating manuals and user inspection.

The following topics are covered, some of these will be very familiar and some may not. Hopefully, the discussion of each topic will be useful and interesting to the reader.

1. *Structures* - linear elastic theory, basic structural theory.
2. *Structural Response* - bending moment, shear force, deflection,
generation of load charts, principle of superposition, dynamic
loading.
3. *Trusses* - types of truss, basic elements of a truss, history of

trusses in entertainment industry, truck packing, trusses available today and their uses, design of elements of a truss, design of connections, robustness.

4. *Design Standards* - latest British and American standards.
5. *Factors of Safety* - what are they, how are they derived, why they are necessary.
6. *Assessment of Loads* - dead load, live load, dynamic loads and dynamic magnification factors, wind loads, loads from fall arrest equipment.
7. *Existing Structures* - what to look for, what to check.
8. *Tower Stability Theory* - discussion about effective heights and relationship with head and base restraint, sway forces and moments, allowable axial loads against height.
9. *Principle of Ground Support* - how it stands up, continuation of tower stability theory.
10. *The Adequacy of a Typical Ground Support Grid* - how to check, worked examples.
11. *Principle and Concepts Behind Roof Structures.*
12. *Wind Loads on Outdoor Structures* - importance, monitoring of wind speeds.
13. *Guy ropes, ground anchors, ballast.*
14. *Stages* - design loads, bracing, sway forces, front of stage barriers.
15. *Operating Manuals* - aims, information within these documents, user information.
16. *User Inspection* - what to do, what to look for.

The photograph on page 13 shows the lighting rig and roof structure built for the Gloria Estefan concert in the Aztec Stadium in Mexico City in 1997. The rig carried 24 tonnes of lighting and associated equipment. But just how did we manage to keep it all in the air? Why did the lighting rig not fall killing the artist and the band? Why did the roof structure not collapse onto the audience? Just how do we do it? I will refer back to this project to show you how each part of the roof and lighting grid was designed to carry the loads safely.

The safety of the performers, the crew and the public are of paramount importance. Safety must be the overriding factor - ahead of monetary issues, ahead of time schedules, ahead of personal egos, ahead of stunning effects...

Lighting rig and roof structure for Gloria Estafan in concert, Aztec Stadium, Mexico City, 1997

The ticket paying public have a right to expect that any show will be entertaining, but more importantly that it should be safe and that the people involved with the production should have used all reasonable care and judgement. This includes the structural engineers who have designed or checked the roof structure, lighting grid or ground support system.

Dr Sam Thorburn, the President of the Institution of Structural Engineers in the UK, made a similar point in his Presidential Address in London in October 1997 when he said:

"The owners of buildings and bridges demand reliability in return for their investment. This expectation presents a challenge to all structural engineers who often are confronted by the requirement in complex situations. Doctors of medicine and members of the legal profession are only expected by society to do their best and, either, the patient has not responded to treatment, or the evidence was insufficient or unreliable. There are no guarantees in medicinal or legal issues, but society expects guarantees from structural engineers."

On the other hand, structural engineers are faced with a number of dilemmas which were aptly summarised by Dr A Dykes at the IStructE in 1976:

"Engineering is the art of modelling materials we do not wholly understand, into shapes we cannot precisely analyse, so as to withstand forces we cannot properly assess, in such a way that the public has no reason to suspect the extent of our ignorance."

This book has been written to provide people with a basic understanding of aluminium structures in order that they can use them safely. Structures can be complicated - I would certainly not suggest that you pick up a text book, read a few pages and then embark on the analysis of a complex structure. One mistake could prove very costly.

1 ALUMINIUM

The majority of the structures and load support equipment such as lighting trusses are fabricated for the entertainment industry from one of a small number of aluminium alloys.

Aluminium is the most abundant metal on earth and is the third most common element. It accounts for 8% of the earth's crust. It is a semi-precious metal which is smelted from bauxite which is plentiful around the world. The smelting process is difficult and uses large amounts of energy, and this is why aluminium is comparatively expensive. The world production of the metal is some 20 million tonnes per year.

Let us consider a number of properties of aluminium and its alloys in order to better understand the material and gauge its suitability for use in both temporary and permanent structures in the entertainment industry.

The coefficient of thermal expansion of aluminium is about twice that of steel. That is to say if an aluminium rod is raised in temperature by a given amount, then it increases in length twice as much as a steel rod of similar dimensions. The temperature required to melt aluminium is 570 to 660°C (1060-1220°F) – about half that of steel. It is a non-magnetic metal, unlike steel.

The thermal conductivity of aluminium is about four times greater than steel. This means that heat is conducted away from the source faster and a larger heat input is required to bring the same amount of aluminium up to a given temperature than for steel. This is an important property when considering how the material behaves in the event of a fire. Where an aluminium structure is subjected to the heat of a fire, the relatively high thermal conductivity enables the heat to be rapidly conducted away from the exposed area. This helps to reduce 'hot spots' where significant localised loss of strength or damage could occur, so extending the serviceability period. It will, however, cause the temperature to rise elsewhere in the structure, providing there is a continuous path along which the heat can travel.

The mechanical properties of aluminium and many of its alloys have been determined at extremely low temperatures – far lower than would be experienced in the natural world. In general, the tensile strength of the pure metal and its alloys is greater at sub zero temperatures than at room temperature. It is understood that none of the alloys suffer from brittleness at low temperatures and there is no transition point below which brittle fracture occurs.

There are major recycling programmes in place around the world and about 5% of the energy required to smelt the primary metal is used in the recycling process.

The strength of the pure metal is low – 60 to 140 N/mm² (8.7 to 20.3 ksi) – according to purity and the amount of cold work to which the metal may have been subjected. By alloying with other elements and by cold working or heat treatment, tensile strengths as high as 600 N/mm² (87 ksi) can be achieved. The principal alloying elements are copper, magnesium, manganese, silicon and zinc.

Aluminium is used in a number of structural alloys which can be classified in two categories as 'heat treatable' and 'non heat treatable'. 'Heat treatable' alloys derive their strength from heat treatment whereas 'non heat treatable' alloys derive enhanced strength only from strain hardening. The properties of these alloys are significantly affected by tempering and vary considerably. Some alloys can be welded easily and others cannot. Some alloys are readily available whereas others are more difficult to source.

There are two main processes uses to weld aluminium elements together: TIG (Tungsten Inert Gas) and MIG (Metal Inert Gas). In the TIG process an alternating current arc is struck between a tungsten electrode and the aluminium work piece. A shroud of inert gas, such as argon, covers the electrode and the weld area. A filler rod is fed into the weld area independently. This method allows close control of the welding process.

The MIG process is somewhat different in that a direct current arc of reverse polarity (with the electrode being positive) shielded by an inert gas shroud is struck between the work piece and a continuously fed aluminium wire electrode which undergoes controlled melting at the tip and so acts as the filler material. The process is good for high speed automatic welding and where larger amounts of heat are required to produce the weld. The process lacks the penetration control which is possible with TIG welding.

It is clear that the selection of the filler material is important to ensure compatibility of alloy and to reduce the possibility of weld cracking.

So why do we use aluminium, what are the advantages and what are the disadvantages over other materials?

The standard sections of aluminium truss and towers which are used in the entertainment can generally be lifted and carried by two people. If steel was used instead of aluminium, the trusses would have a tendency to corrode or rust which would be unsightly, and most likely be heavier than an equivalent aluminium truss.

There are also some downsides to the use of aluminium. The effects of welding need to be very carefully considered during the design process. If you make a mistake you can't simply weld another bit on as it may make the structure weaker. We will discuss weld effects in more detail shortly.

Large deflections may also be a problem with aluminium structures in some instances. Again we will talk about this in more detail.

Common aluminium alloys do have a tendency to become damaged quite easily when subjected to abuse. For example, the chords often lose a significant percentage of their cross sectional area when the trusses are dragged along the floor. The level of damage largely depends how much care is taken in use and on the choice of alloy.

The nature of aluminium is such that it does suffer more than (say) steel would under the same treatment. However, if the equipment is not mistreated or overstressed and handled and transported with an element of care, then it should provide many years of service.

The alloy which is generally used for the manufacture of structural systems in the UK is 6082-T6 aluminium alloy. This alloy was formerly known as HE-30-TF. 6082-T6 material is not readily available in the US where 6061-T6 aluminium alloy is used. It has very similar properties to the 6082-T6 material used in the UK.

6061-T6 and 6082-T6 are heat treatable alloys with a durability rating of 'B', which means that surface protection such as paint is only needed where the truss is used in severe urban, industrial or marine environments. It is therefore considered that surface protection is not required for use in the entertainment industry. However, if the trusses are subjected to a salty atmosphere, then they should be rinsed on a regular basis as required.

It should be noted that some oxidisation of the alloy will take place when it used outdoors. Some minor pitting is likely, but this should not affect the structural performance of the members.

The T6 temper condition means that the alloy is solution treated and artificially aged to improve the strength of the material. The proof stress, tensile strength and hardness of the alloy are therefore increased. The effects of tempering are significantly reduced by welding as the material in the Heat Affected Zone is softened and is reduced strength.

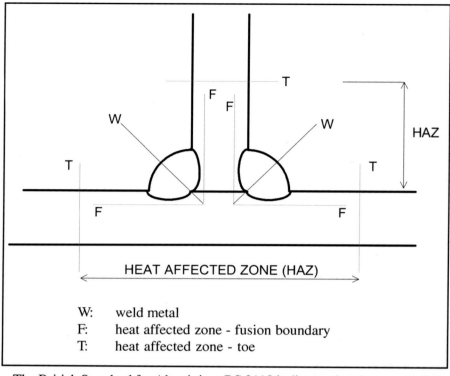

HEAT AFFECTED ZONE (HAZ)

W: weld metal
F: heat affected zone - fusion boundary
T: heat affected zone - toe

The British Standard for Aluminium BS 8118 indicates that the extent of the softening due to welding varies from aluminium alloy to aluminium alloy. This reduction in strength is typically between 20% and 80%. The standard states that the strength of the 6082-T6 or 6061-T6 alloys is reduced by some 50% within a given distance from the weld.

The width of the heat affected zone is governed by the amount of heat required to produce the weld and how easily the heat is dissipated. The thickness of the connecting plies – the thickness of the tubes which are to be joined – therefore determines the extent of the heat affected zone. It requires more heat input to produce a weld using thicker materials and hence the heat affected zone has a greater width. If the heat affected zone of one weld overlaps that of another weld, the strength is not reduced further than 50%.

In America, the Aluminum Association standard takes a much more simplistic approach. The standard provides allowable stresses for the parent metal and the material within 1 inch (25.4mm) of the weld. This approach is reminiscent of that taken in CP 118 which was the British Standard that was superceded by BS 8118.

So we now have information on how welding effects the aluminium components in the Gloria Estafan roof and lighting grid. But how does this help? Firstly, we need some more information and a better understanding of structural theory.

2 BASIC STRUCTURAL THEORY

The basic philosophy in linear elastic theory is that the materials in the structure will remain elastic when the structure is subjected to the design working loads. Only when the structure is overloaded will the elements become overstressed and become plastic. That is to say when the load is removed the element will not return to its original size and permanent deformation results. Let us look into this in more detail as it the basis of the analysis of the structure.

The fundamental experimental law on which linear elastic theory is based was discovered by Robert Hooke in 1678. When subjected to a uniaxial loading it was found that for certain materials the extension was proportional to the applied load. If a rod of a linear elastic material with a uniform cross section is loaded axially, the stress is uniform over the cross section and would be equal to the load divided by the cross sectional area.

The axial strain is the extension divided by the original length, so Hooke's Law can be written as:

stress is proportional to strain

$$\sigma_{xx} \propto \varepsilon_{xx}$$

The constant of proportionality, E, which will vary from one elastic material to another can be introduced - this is known as Young's Modulus, or the modulus of elasticity.

stress equals Young's Modulus multiplied by strain

$$\sigma_{xx} = E \, \varepsilon_{xx}$$

If P is the load applied to a rod of cross sectional area A

the stress $\sigma_{xx} = P \, / \, A$

Suppose the rod is of length l and extends by an amount e

then strain $\varepsilon_{xx} = e \, / \, I$

Substituting in the earlier equation

$$P \, / \, A = E \, e \, / \, I$$

or e = $\dfrac{P\,l}{A\,E}$

Young's Modulus is stress divided by strain where strain is elongation divided by the original length, where the stress and strain are measured in the elastic part of the graph. Young's Modulus is therefore the gradient of the graph of stress versus strain.

Proof stress is the stress at which a non-proportional elongation equal to a specified percentage of the original gauge length occurs. When a proof stress is specified, the non proportional elongation should be stated e.g. 0.2%.

If a rod of linear elastic material with a uniform cross section is loaded axially, the stress is uniform over the cross section and would be equal to the

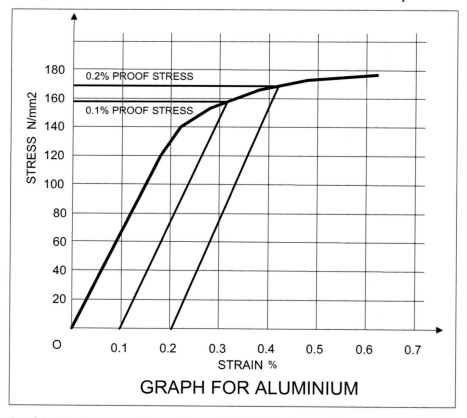

Load / extension curve, illustrating method of deriving proof stress

load divided by the area of the cross section. Axial strain is the extension divided by the original length.

Typical values of Young's Modulus for mild steel and aluminium are approximately 210 and 70 kN/mm² (30,300 and 10,100 ksi) respectively. Therefore, it can be seen that for a given force on a given cross section, an aluminium element would extend, or compress, about three times as much as a comparable steel element.

If careful measurements are made on the specimen being considered in the test, it will be found that the dimensions of cross section will also change when the load is applied. The strain in both the y and z directions is proportional to the strain in the x direction but opposite in sign. The constant of proportionality n is referred to as Poisson's Ratio.

That is to say as the specimen elongates in the direction of the tension it contracts in the other two directions. This can be seen in many places in everyday life. We will come back to this phenomenon later.

The behaviour of aluminium under load, like steel and most other metals, is linear elastic up to the elastic limit. Above this point the response to loads is plastic - the recovery is not complete when the load is relieved and there is permanent deformation when the load is taken off. When a material has reached the elastic limit it is said to have reached yield but has not fractured. More load can be added above yield up to a point where the material fails.

The elastic modulus of aluminium and its alloys is about one third that of steel. The elastic deflection is therefore correspondingly greater which, in some circumstances, can be an advantage. For example, it allows a better distribution of stress in a composite structure and minimises the effect of any slight lack of fit in components parts. When an aluminium structure is loaded under shock conditions, its greater resilience enables it to absorb more energy than a corresponding steel structure.

Well, that sounds a bit complicated to me - so a diagram may help illustrate the point.

The following diagrams show the relationship between stress and strain for mild steel and aluminium. You will see that the portion OA is linear - a straight line. At A there is a yield point with a sudden drop in stress to a lower yield point B. This is followed by what is termed the plastic range, BD where there is a large increase in strain for a small increase in stress. Thereafter the stress increases more rapidly with work hardening until the ultimate stress is reached at E where failure occurs.

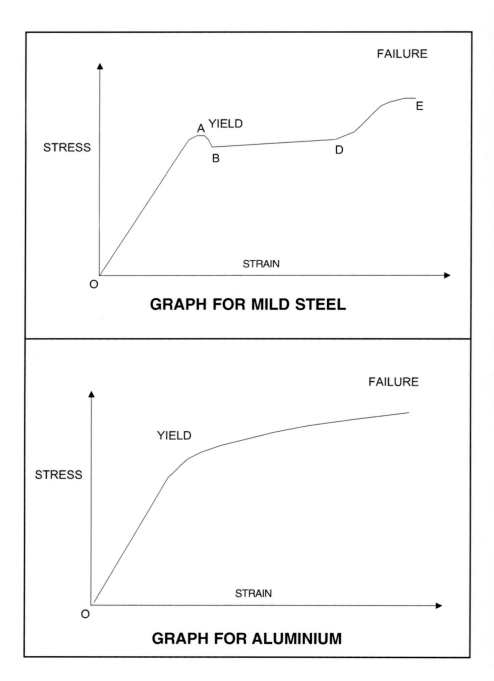

GRAPH FOR MILD STEEL

GRAPH FOR ALUMINIUM

You can see the differences between the behaviour of steel and aluminium under load. After the elastic limit has been reached, the aluminium specimen elongates steadily with little increase in load before failure is reached.

We mentioned Young's Modulus earlier and talked about strain being the extension divided by the original length. We can now see that as the chords elongate or compress under load and that deflection of the truss is linked to strain. We also know that stress is linked to strain by Young's Modulus and that stress is linked to load. So now we can see how load is linked to deflection.

The deflection, which is the amount of bending of the aluminium sections, is about three times more than steel, for the same section size and loading configuration, and hence the structures generally become very distorted before they fracture. This could well be the reason why there have not been more accidents within the entertainment industry. When people see excessive deflection and distortion or twisting in trusses, they do tend to stop adding more load!

Deflection should not be confused with a phenomenon called creep. If an element is subjected to a load for a very protracted period at intermediate temperatures, there may be a slow plastic strain, that is to say that the material will gradually extend. We can see from this graph that for material which is stressed to about 50N/mm² (7.25 ksi) for a period of 1000 hours at 200°C (392°F), the extension will be approximately 0.2%.

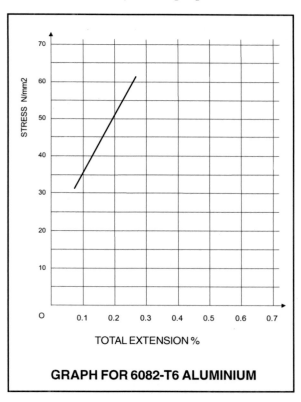

GRAPH FOR 6082-T6 ALUMINIUM

This deformation will not recover when the load is removed. Creep is greater at higher temperatures for most alloys above 300°C (572°F). Creep is generally not significant for the material used in the entertainment industry as the temperatures of the structures rarely reach such values. There may be localised hot spots, but because the material is such a good conductor, the heat is dissipated.

We should, perhaps, also consider the variation in strength of aluminium with temperature. This diagram shows the variation of tensile strength with temperature.

It is important to note that these tensile strengths shown are for material at those temperatures and not the strengths after cooling. Some recovery in strength can be expected after the removal of the heat source.

We can see that the strength of the material which we use is not significantly affected in the normal ranges of temperature in which structures are expected to be used. However, one should note that the strength of aluminium would be severely compromised in the event of a fire. See graph opposite.

So we now have a relationship between load and response for a single member and have discounted the effects of creep, temperature and understand about elastic response, yield and failure.

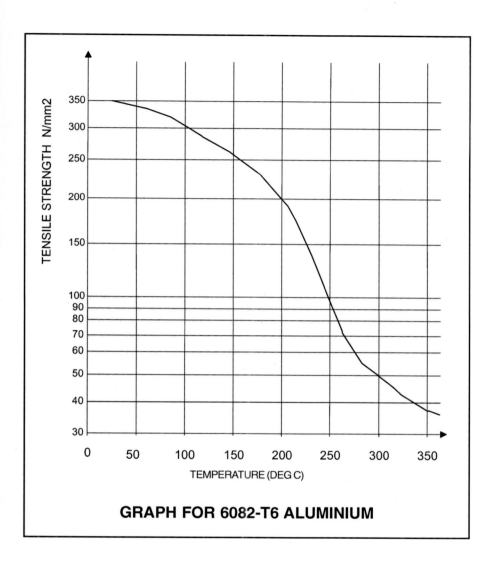

GRAPH FOR 6082-T6 ALUMINIUM

3 STRUCTURAL RESPONSE

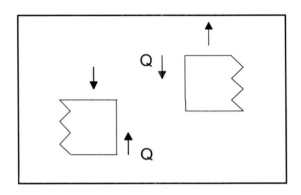

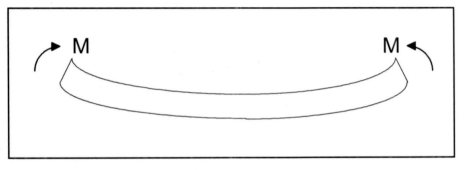

"For every action, there is an equal and opposite reaction" -
Sir Isaac Newton

These diagrams above show what bending moment, axial force and shear force are.

Now let us consider a simply supported beam which is subjected to two point loads, P1 and P2. One end of the beam is restrained and one end is free to travel across the ground.

When we consider any particular section of the beam, the bending moments, shear forces and axial forces must balance or we would have a mechanism. To keep each portion of the beam in equilibrium the following forces will be required: an axial force F, a transverse force Q, known as the shear force, and a bending moment M.

The aim of all structural design is to produce a structure that is capable of carrying the specified forces with an adequate margin of safety.

When a system of forces is applied to a structure, it will be ultimately resisted by reactions onto the structure at the positions of support. This follows one of Newton's Laws which states that "For every action, there is an equal and opposite reaction".

The response of the structure to transfer the applied forces to the foundations takes the form of bending moments, shear forces, axial compression or tension and torsion in the elements of the structure. Therefore design can be extremely complicated.

For the time being the discussion will be limited to a simple straight beam where the applied loads and reactions lie in a single plane which contains the centroidal axis of the beam. That is to say, there is no twisting or torsion because the loads and supports line through the centre of stiffness. It is assumed that the beam is stable when these loads are applied.

Imagine the beam to be split in two at XX. Then the free body diagram will be as shown below.

To keep each portion of the beam in equilibrium the following forces will be required: an axial force F, a transverse force Q, known as the shear force, and a bending moment M.

For equilibrium at the section, the corresponding forces in each section must

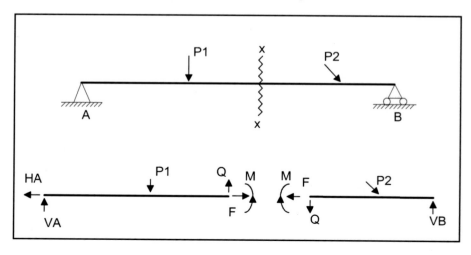

oppose each other. For example, if there is a clockwise moment M shown on the right hand side, this must be opposed by an anti-clockwise moment M on the left hand side. The values of these forces can be determined from the load applied to the beam and the values of the reactions.

The axial force is the resultant of all components of applied loads and re-actions acting parallel to the axis of the beam at the point considered. Tensile forces are generally taken as positive and compressive forces as negative.

If a beam is in equilibrium and we imagine it to be cut vertically, it will be necessary to apply forces normal to the axis of the beam, lying in the section, to maintain equilibrium. These forces Q are known as shear forces. You will see that the forces on either side of the section are equal and opposite.

If the resultant of all the forces acting on the left hand portion of the beam is downward then a force Q would have to act upwards. For the right hand portion of the beam the resultant force and the shear force will act in opposite senses.

The bending moment is the sum of the moments taken about an axis normal to the plane of the applied loads and reactions, and passing through the centroidal axis of the beam at the point considered. The centroidal axis is the axis which passes through the centre of gravity. The bending moment will be taken as positive when it is 'sagging'. This means that the beam will be concave - the fibres at the top will be compressed and those at the bottom edge will be extended.

Structures generally comprise more than one member - these are structural systems. A structural system will respond to the applied forces, in the form of bending moment, axial force and shear force in the component elements of that structure.

There are two basic principles to analyse simple beams and structures. These are the called the resolution of forces and the balance of moments at any one point in the structure.

At any one point within a structure, the total forces resolved in one direction should be zero. That is to say the sum of the forces in one direction should be equal and opposite to the sum of the forces in the opposing direction. If they were not, the point would move as there was nett force on that point.

The component of a force resolved into a different direction is equal the force multiplied by the cosine of the angle between the direction of the force and the direction under consideration. This is shown in the following diagram.

This method is particularly useful. A good example would be the computa-

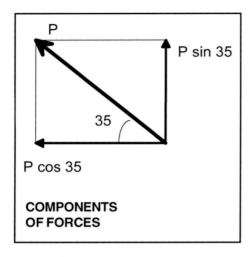

P

P sin 35

35

P cos 35

**COMPONENTS
OF FORCES**

tion of the forces in the chains in a bridle and the compression in the element being lifted. Assume that the weight to be lifted is 1000 kg and the chain are at 30 degrees to the vertical and that the bridle chains are the same length. The angle of both chains to the vertical is the same. Let the force in each chain be T1 and T2.

If we consider the point at the top support where both chains are attached, there are three forces acting: the force in each of the two chains and the vertical force to the support. If we resolve the forces horizontally by multi-plying the force in the chain by the cosine of the angle of the chain to the horizontal, we find

T1 cosine 60 = T2 cosine 60
and the force in each chain is therefore equal.

If we resolve the forces vertically by multiplying the force in each chain by the cosine of the angle to the vertical, we find

T1 cosine 30 + T2 cosine 30 = 1000 kg
but the force in each chain is the same. Let this value be T.

2 T cosine 30 = 1000
T = 577 kg

Now consider the point where the chain meets the spreader beam. Let the compression in the spreader beam be C. Resolving horizontally, we get

T cosine 60 = C
C = 289 kg

If we have an unequal bridle, then we have a more complex problem. But again, we can break it down into a series of equations at each point.

The tension in each leg of the bridle may be different. So let the tensions be T1 and T2 and the angle between each leg and vertical be $\theta 1$ and $\theta 2$.

If we resolve the forces vertically at the intersection of the bridle legs with the weight then we obtain the following equation:

$$T1 \text{ cosine } \theta 1 + T2 \text{ cosine } \theta 2 = W \qquad \text{......... Equation 1}$$

If we then resolve the forces horizontally at the same point, then we obtain:

$$T1 \text{ sine } \theta 1 = T2 \text{ sine } \theta 2 \qquad \text{......... Equation 2}$$

We can then solve these simultaneous equations to determine the force in each leg of the bridle.

Let us consider a worked example to illustrate the point.

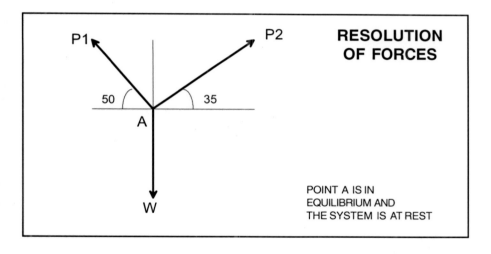

Resolving forces in vertical direction

$$P1 \sin 50 + P2 \sin 35 = W \qquad \text{.......... Equation 1}$$

Resolving forces in horizontal direction

$$P1 \cos 50 = P2 \cos 35 \qquad \text{.......... Equation 2}$$

Reorganising equation 2

$$P1 = P2 \cos 35 / \cos 50 = 1.274 \ P2 \qquad \text{.......... Equation 3}$$

Substituting in equation 1

$1.274\ P2 \sin 50 + P2 \sin 35 = W$

$0.976\ P2 + 0.574\ P2 = 1.55\ P2 = W$

$P2 = 0.645\ W$

Substituting in equation 2

$P1 \sin 50 + 0.645\ W \sin 35 = W$

$0.766\ P1 + 0.645 \times 0.574\ W = W$

$P1 = ((1 - 0.37) / 0.766)\ W$

$P1 = 0.822\ W$

Checking in equation 2

$0.822\ W \cos 50 = 0.645\ W \cos 35$

$0.528W = 0.528\ W$ OK

Checking in equation 1

$0.822\ W \sin 50 + 0.645\ W \sin 35 = W$

$0.63\ W + 0.37\ W = W$ OK

<u>$P1 = 0.822\ W$</u>   <u>$P2 = 0.645\ W$</u>

It is sometimes difficult to determine the angles of the legs of the bridles to the vertical whilst rigging the point. So the relationship between the angle and the vertical and horizontal distances from the point to the support locations is useful.

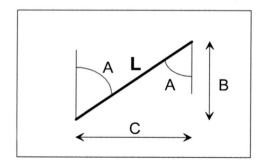

From basic geometry, we know that the length of the bridle is

$$L^2 = A^2 + B^2 \qquad L = \sqrt{(A^2 + B^2)}$$

Tangent A = C / B

Cosine A = B / L

Sine A = C / L

So we can now substitute the values of sine and cosine of the angle in earlier equations with these figures to determine the tension in the legs of the bridle.

The other method of analysis is to check the balance of moments at any position along a beam. The moments must be in equilibrium for the structure to be stable at that position. We can use this method to determine the support reactions at each end of a beam or truss. If we consider each end of the beam in turn, then we eliminate the other variable which we are trying to determine. This is shown in the following diagram.

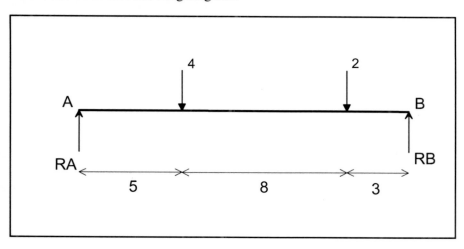

The beam is in equilibrium and therefore does not rotate.

If we consider point A, the anticlockwise moments must equal the clockwise moments.

$$(4 \times 5) + (2 \times (5 + 8)) = RB \times (5 + 8 + 3)$$

$$RB = 2.875$$

If we consider point B, the anticlockwise moments must equal the clockwise moments.

$$(3 \times 2) + (4 \times (3 + 8)) = RA \times (5 + 8 + 3)$$

$$RA = 3.125$$

To check these figures are correct, consider the beam as a whole. The beam does not move up or down, so the total of the vertical forces must equal zero. The reactions are upwards, so they have the opposite sign to the applied forces which are downwards.

$$RA + 4 + 2 + RB = -3.125 + 4 + 2 - 2.875 = 0 \qquad \text{OK}$$

If a member extends over a support and has a free end, it is known as a cantilever. The bending moment over the support will be of opposite sign and is known as 'hogging'.

If a single truss is supported at each end and a load applied, then the bending moment and shear force within the truss transfers the load back to the support positions. A bending moment results in compression and tension in the top and bottom chords respectively in a truss. The diagram above shows how.

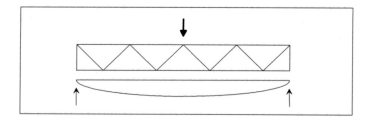

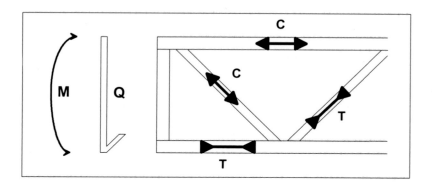

We can plot the values of the bending moment and shear force along the length of the beam to produce diagrams such as this:

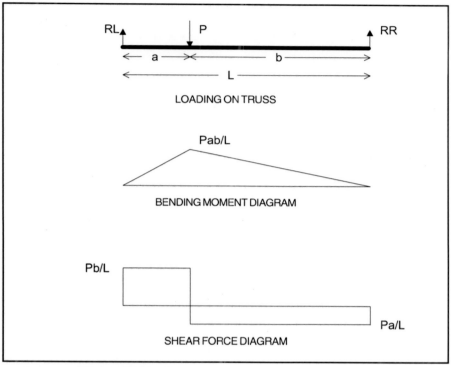

where: P is applied load
          a is distance from left hand end
          b is distance from right hand end
          L is simply supported span
          RL is reaction at left hand end = Pb/L
          RR is reaction at right hand end = Pa/L

The bending moment in the truss results in the deflection. This cannot be avoided - structures do deflect under their self-weight and when loads are applied - the deflections may be very small but they do exist.

In the UK, forces are generally measured in Newtons or kilonewtons (one thousand Newtons). Let us consider that a tonne is a measure of weight and not of mass. There are approximately 9.81 kilonewtons in a tonne. Those of you who are particularly quick on mental arithmetic will see that a Newton is approximately the weight of a large apple. I'm sure there is a joke in there somewhere about Sir Isaac Newton sitting under a tree when an apple falls on his head and he 'discovers' gravity!!

A bending moment is measured in kilonewton metres. 1 kilonewton metre is the moment of one kilonewton acting with a lever arm of one metre. It is therefore a measure of leverage. 1 tonne metre is about 9.81 kilonewton metres. Moments are also known as couples - that is two equal forces acting in opposite directions separated by a given distance - sounds like marriage really. So, just as in life, "every couple has its moment".

We can now see that for a given bending moment, the further apart the chords the less force there is in each chord. Conversely, if the force in the chord remains constant, the further apart the chords the greater the allowable bending moment.

Stress is force per unit area and is usually measured in Newtons per square millimetre. Deflections are generally measured in millimetres.

In America, they use a different measurement system - the imperial or F.P.S. system - the one we discarded in the UK some years ago.

The units of force in the US are kips which are kilopounds i.e. a thousands pounds of weight - roughly half a tonne.

Feet kips for the measurement of bending moment. One foot kip is therefore the leverage of a thousand pounds at 1 foot.

The measurement of deflection is usually inches and the measurement of stress is ksi which is kilopounds per square inch.

Now we have a basic understanding of bending moments, shear forces and deflection and their units of measurement.

The uniformly distributed load is the load which is evenly distributed along the entire length of the truss as series of point loads at the nodes or panel points.

A central point load is one load which is positioned at a node or panel point at the centre of the truss.

A third point load is a pair of point loads which are positioned at a node or panel point a third of the way along the truss from each end.

A quarter point load is three point loads which are positioned at a node or panel point a quarter of the way along the truss from each end and at the centre.

These distributions of loads result in bending moments and shear forces which vary along the span and which can be put in diagram form as demonstrated on the following pages:

RESPONSE TO UNIFORMLY DISTRIBUTED LOAD

LOAD CONFIGURATION - U.D.L.

W (total)

L

BENDING MOMENT DIAGRAM

$$\frac{WL}{8}$$

SHEAR FORCE DIAGRAM

$$\frac{W}{2}$$

$$\frac{W}{2}$$

DEFLECTION

$$\frac{5\,W\,L^3}{384\,E\,I}$$

RESPONSE TO CENTRAL POINT LOAD

LOAD CONFIGURATION - C.P.L.

P

L

=   =

BENDING MOMENT DIAGRAM

$$\dfrac{PL}{4}$$

SHEAR FORCE DIAGRAM

$$\dfrac{P}{2}$$

$$\dfrac{P}{2}$$

DEFLECTION

$$\dfrac{P\,L^3}{48\,E\,I}$$

RESPONSE TO THIRD POINT LOAD

LOAD CONFIGURATION - T.P.L.

BENDING MOMENT DIAGRAM

$$\frac{PL}{3}$$

SHEAR FORCE DIAGRAM

P

P

DEFLECTION

$$\frac{23\,P\,L^3}{648\,E\,I}$$

RESPONSE TO QUARTER POINT LOAD

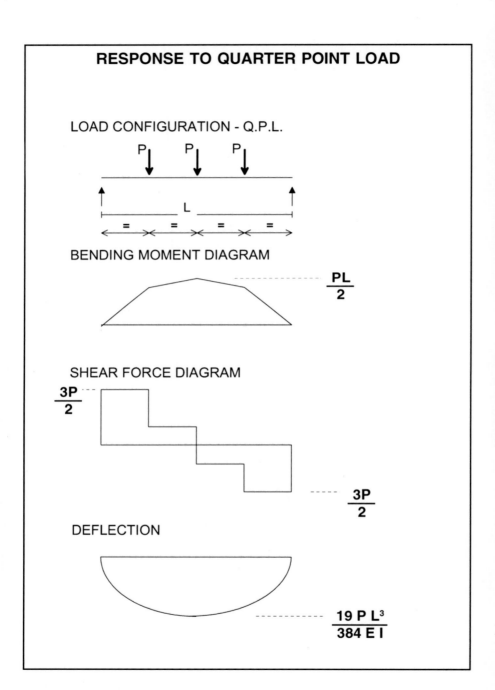

LOAD CONFIGURATION - Q.P.L.

P   P   P

L

= ⤬ = ⤬ = ⤬ =

BENDING MOMENT DIAGRAM

$$\frac{PL}{2}$$

SHEAR FORCE DIAGRAM

$$\frac{3P}{2}$$

$$\frac{3P}{2}$$

DEFLECTION

$$\frac{19\,P\,L^3}{384\,E\,I}$$

These are standard diagrams that are used in engineering circles. I will not elaborate further on how these figures are determined as this is outside the scope of this book. You will note that the position of maximum bending moment always occurs when the shear force is zero or when the line on the shear force diagram passes through zero. This is an important feature to note and is very useful as we shall find out shortly.

Bending moments are determined at any location by theoretically splitting the beam and taking moments at that point. Shear forces are determined by resolution of forces at that point. We will see an example of this shortly.

Once we have found the maximum allowable bending moments and shear forces in a truss we can establish allowable load charts. The load charts take into consideration the self-weight of the truss and they plot the allowable load on a truss for a particular type of load for a range of spans. Clearly, there are numerous configurations of loading to which the truss could be subjected and hence it is not possible to cover each and every case. Therefore, a number of idealistic and simplistic configurations are analysed in the structural calculations and manufacturers produce allowable load charts for the truss to assist the client or user to use the equipment safely.

Load charts are generally produced for four very simplistic and idealistic loading scenarios - namely uniformly distributed load (UDL), central point

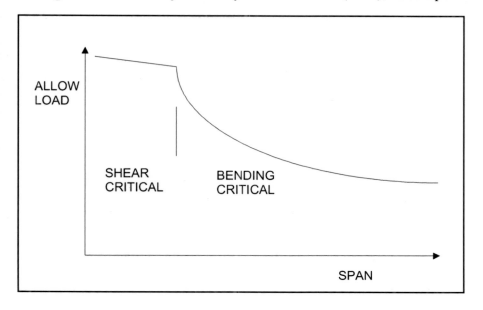

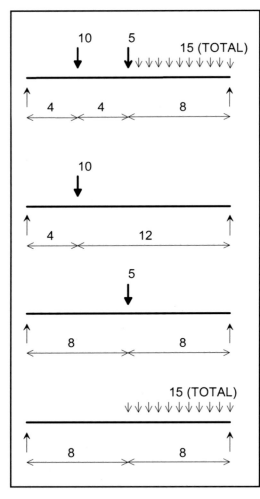

load (CPL), third point load (TPL) and quarter point load (QPL). They are simple to use.

This is a typical example of a load chart of allowable load against span. You can see two distinct areas of the graph - one where the diagonals are critical - the truss is said to be shear critical and the other where the chords or connections are critical - the truss is said to be bending critical.

The static payload is defined as the static equivalent loading imposed upon the structure. This must include the weight of any luminaires, associated equipment, rigging trusses and their fixings, fastenings and hoisting equipment, together with the electrical cables.

The distribution of payload across the width of the truss should be balanced so that no torsion or undue twisting is induced in the truss. The loads should be balanced when the truss is considered as a whole or over any particular section of truss so that the truss does not twist.

The distribution of the payload on the structure is crucial to the stability of the system as a whole. Check calculations shall be carried out by the user for individual circumstances. The structures should be re-analysed for more complex distributions of load and the actual maximum bending moment and shear force determined for that distribution of load and compared with the allowable maximum values given in the structural calculations to determine if the truss is adequate.

So how do we determine the maximum bending moment and shear forces for more complex load distributions?

Let us consider how to analyse the load configuration shown in the diagrams.

The maximum bending moment and shear force can be determined by 'the principal of superposition'. This principle states that, for a linear elastic system in which changes in geometry are small, the effect **m** due to a cause **M** can be added to the effect **n** due to a cause **N**. Thus the result will be the same as the effect **m+n** due to a cause **M+N**. The principle is not valid if the material of the system is non elastic or has exceeded its yield point, or if the geometry of the structure changes appreciably as the load is applied.

Obviously, the geometry of all structures must change slightly as loads are applied. Individual members will extend or contract resulting in points on the structure deflecting. The changes in the majority of cases are small and can be neglected in applying this principle.

Applying the principle of superposition the effect of a number of forces is assumed to be equal to the sum of the effects when each force is applied individually. So the values of bending moment and shear force can be determined at a given position for the various loads and then summated to give a total bending moment or shear force for that position.

As mentioned earlier, for simply supported spans, the maximum bending moment occurs at the position of zero shear force. For those who are particularly interested here is a diagram and some formulae to prove it.

The drawing below shows a small element dx cut from a beam. It is loaded by a force on the top surface, of average intensity p per unit length, acting upwards. To keep the element in equilibrium it is necessary to add both shear

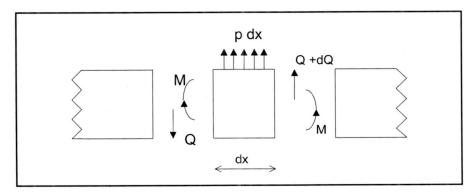

forces and bending moments. These will change in value from one side of the element to the other. As the load acts in a positive y direction, it is considered positive.

resolving vertically

$$Q + dQ = Q - p\ dx$$

thus

$$\frac{dQ}{dx} = -p \qquad \text{equation 1}$$

Taking moments about the right hand edge, omitting the term involving the load as a second order quantity

$$M + dM + Q\ dx = M$$

thus

$$\frac{dM}{dx} = -Q \qquad \text{equation 2}$$

Making use of this equation we can express equation 1 as

$$\frac{d^2M}{dx^2} = p \qquad \text{equation 3}$$

Equation 2 shows that that if the shear force is negative then the rate of change of bending moment is positive, so that the value of bending moment is increasing. Also the value of the bending moment will be a maximum or a minimum when the shear force is zero. Exception to this would be when there is a sudden change in the value of a bending moment due to the application of a couple.

Equation 2 can be integrated such that

$$M_2 - M_1 = \int_{x_1}^{x_2} -Q\ dx$$

Thus the change in moment between any two points is given by the area of the shear force diagram between the two points. An exception to this would be if a couple were applied between the two points considered.

The position of zero force is quite easily determined and the maximum bending moment calculated. The maximum shear force should also determined - this usually occurs at the supports.

This may sound a bit complicated and here is a worked example with two point loads and a uniformly distributed load (UDL).

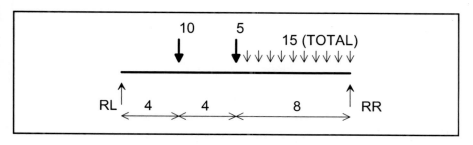

$16 \times RR = (10 \times 4) + (5 \times 8) + (15 \times 12)$

$RR = 16.25$ kN

$16 \times RL = (15 \times 4) + (5 \times 8) + (10 \times 12)$

$RL = 13.75$ kN

Check $10 + 5 + 15 = 30$ $16.25 + 13.75 = 30$ OK

zero shear at centre

Taking moments about left hand end

Max bending moment $= (13.75 \times 8) - (10 \times 4) - (5 \times 8) = 30$ kNm

   Now that we have looked at bending and shear in the beam, we should consider how much it will deflect.
   The deflection of the truss due to the load can be <u>estimated</u> from the formulae given below:

<u>Uniformly distributed load</u> $d = \dfrac{5 \; WL^3}{384 \; E \, I}$

<u>Central point load</u> $d = \dfrac{PL^3}{48 \; E \, I}$

<u>Third point load</u> $d = \dfrac{23 \; PL^3}{648 \; E \, I}$

Quarter point load $\qquad d = \dfrac{19 \ PL^3}{384 \ E \ I}$

where: W is the total superimposed load on the truss
L is the span of the truss between supports
P is the superimposed point load
E is Young's Modulus for aluminium = 70000 N/mm² (10,100 ksi)
I is the moment of inertia of the truss (defined in structural calculations but is essentially a measure of the stiffness of the truss)

Note!   *Need to add deflection due to self weight.*
Note!   *Need to consider deflection due to slippage in connection.*

The deflection of a simply supported beam due to a particular load configuration can be <u>estimated</u> from the formulae given above.

Firstly, the bending moment in the truss should be determined and the equivalent uniformly distributed load be determined which would result in that bending moment. The deflection is then determined using the formula for the deflection using that uniform load.

The deflection due to the self-weight should be added to the deflection due to the applied load to get the total deflection. Clearly, as the self weight is a uniformly distributed load the deflection due to the self-weight is determined from the first formula.

It should be noted that the deflection can only be estimated for structures which comprise a number of individual components as some deflection of the truss is often associated with tolerances in the connections, flexing of the end plates of the truss, extension or compression of the elements of the truss and the like.

If the distribution of load is complex then we need a quick way of determining the deflection. The deflection can be estimated from the maximum bending moment as follows in this example.

If the total bending moment (including that due to the self weight) is calculated to be 25 kNm for a 15 metres span and the I value of the truss taken from the structural calculations is 240 x 10⁶ mm⁴, then the deflection can be estimated as follows:

$\qquad M = W \ L \ / \ 8 \qquad$ where M is the bending moment in kNm,
$\qquad\qquad\qquad\qquad\qquad$ W is the total load in kN

$$\text{L is the span in metres}$$

$$25 \quad = \quad W \times 15 / 8$$

$$W \quad = \quad 13.33 \text{ kN}$$

$$d \quad = \quad \frac{5 \ WL^3}{384 \ E \ I}$$

$$= \quad \frac{5 \times 13.33 \times 10^3 \times 15000^3}{384 \times 70000 \times 240 \times 10^6} = 34.87 \text{ mm}$$

This is an example for the Americans and those who are not familiar with SI units:

If the bending moment is calculated to be 18.4 feet-kips for a 50 feet span and the I value of the truss taken from the structural calculations is 576 in^4, then the deflection can be estimated as follows.

$$M \quad = \quad W L / 8$$

$$18.4 \quad = \quad W \times 50 / 8$$

$$W \quad = \quad 2.944 \text{ kips}$$

$$d \quad = \quad \frac{5 \ WL^3}{384 \ E \ I}$$

$$= \quad \frac{5 \times 2.944 \times 10^3 \times 50^3 \times 12^3}{384 \times 10100000 \times 576} = 1.423 \text{ in}$$

Generally, this method gives an answer within a few percent of the actual deflection.

If the truss is hoisted when it is loaded using chain motors or similar or moved during the show, then account needs to be taken by the user of the 'snatch' loads associated with these types of motors. What is known as a dynamic magnification factor is used to reduce the allowable static payload. The value of this dynamic magnification factor is usually defined by the user as it depends on the type of motor used and the type of controller. Clearly, if the motor has a slow start and stop then a different reduction factor should be used from one where the motor starts and stops very abruptly.

If some items are supported by a truss which moves then the static equivalent load is greater than the actual weight of the items. This is because of the acceleration and deceleration of the items.

This can be seen when a weight is supported by a piece of elastic. The elastic stretches a certain distance when the load and the support are stationary. When the support is moved abruptly upwards, the elastic stretches - the load has increased.

So we can now compare the loads on the rigging plot for the Gloria Estafan show with the allowable load charts. We can also check for a variety of load configurations to determine if a truss is adequate.

Let us now take some time to look at trusses and their design in more detail.

4 TRUSSES AND TOWER SECTIONS

We have talked about aluminium, applied loads, bending moments, shear forces, deflection - so how do these relate to the trusses and tower modules and just how have we arrived at the types of trusses which we use today? It is worth considering where it all started.

Pipe battens were used to carry lights in theatres and other venues, and there became a need for these battens to span greater distances without undue deformation. After some lateral thinking by some of the early pioneers of the industry, ladder trusses and subsequently box trusses evolved.

A number of theatres built in the early twentieth century were equipped with bars from which lights and scenery could be suspended, and these can be seen in many towns and cities around the world. Most of the early concerts were very small by today's standards and only involved a small number of lights. They did not take place in well-equipped theatres or purpose-built venues but were frequently staged in multi-purpose buildings which have very little or no provision for hanging equipment.

There was, therefore, a need to build structures within these buildings which would carry the lights above and around the stage. The difference between theatre and concerts at that time was that the theatre shows tended to run for a period of at least a week or two, whereas a concert usually lasted one or two nights at most.

Where the concert was part of a tour, it would be necessary to install these structures in a number of venues and they would essentially be the same on each occasion. The concert tour would move town to town and city to city on consecutive nights.

Six lamp pipe batten

Clearly, it would inappropriate and very expensive to fabricate these structures specifically for each venue. So what was required were structures which could be erected quickly, readily demountable and which could be moved easily from one venue to another.

Various people developed their own solutions to the problem of hanging lighting overhead instead of attaching them to vertical poles which were arranged around the stage. These developments took place in the early 1970s. The basic design of these structures took the form of trusses which were copied from antennae. The chords of the trusses were made larger and thicker than those used on the antennae as they were prone to damage.

The early trusses were manufactured from steel and aluminium, however steel was not favoured because of its weight and tendency to corrode. Aluminium trusses were preferred as each truss could be easily lifted by one or two people and was not prone to rust.

The problem of having to attach and detach the lighting fixtures at each venue was tackled by developing trusses where the lights could travel inside the truss and then moved so that they hung below the bottom of it for the show. This type of truss was originally known as the pre-rigged or Par truss.

A truss is an early type of structural form. It was not invented specifically for the entertainment industry.

Typical Types of Truss

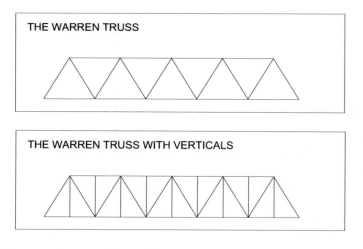

THE WARREN TRUSS

THE WARREN TRUSS WITH VERTICALS

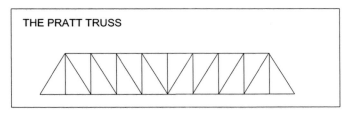

THE PRATT TRUSS

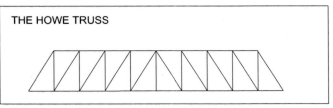

THE HOWE TRUSS

THE K TRUSS

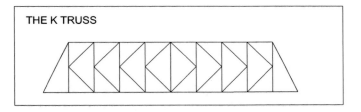

There are many types of truss structures and some examples are shown here:

The *Warren Truss* with parallel chords and regular diagonals. The force in the diagonals alternates between tension and compression.

The *Warren Truss with parallel chords, verticals and regular diagonals*. The vertical members transfer vertical forces from the chords to the intersection of the diagonals (a node or panel point)

The *Pratt Truss* with parallel chords, verticals, and regular diagonals which are inclined in opposite ways, either side of the centre line. Here the diagonals are generally in tension.

The *Howe Truss* with parallel chords, verticals, and regular diagonals which are inclined in opposite ways, either side of the centre line. But in this case the diagonals are generally in compression.

Finally, the *K Truss* with parallel chords, verticals and diagonals which are in the form of a series of Ks either side of the centre line. This layout is often used where the truss is particularly deep where the length of the diagonals would be result in very large sections being used to resist the compression forces.

Some of these layouts will be familiar to those of you who observe the built environment.

The diagram below shows the principal elements of a typical truss that is used in the entertainment industry. It takes the form of a number of chords which are laced with diagonals. A node point (or panel point) on a truss structure is defined as the intersection of the chords with the lacing members such as the diagonal and vertical elements of the truss.

The chords on standard trusses in the entertainment industry are two inch diameter, scaffold size or schedule pipe to facilitate the attachment of fixings for luminaires and the like. The chords are generally larger in size and cross sectional area on trusses which are required to span long distances and carry heavy loads.

Ladder trusses, triangular trusses and box trusses have two, three and four chords respectively.

Truck packing was also a consideration in the early design of trusses. Many of the shows were promoted on a very tight budget and saving on transportation was, as is the case today, a high priority. Just how many of these trusses could be packed into a truck?

Typical internal dimensions of an ISO sea container and a typical articulated truck in the UK are 2.330 m wide by 2.197 m high and 2.345 m wide by 2.36 m high respectively. It is worth noting that the opening for the doors of the container is slightly less than the internal dimensions. One feature of

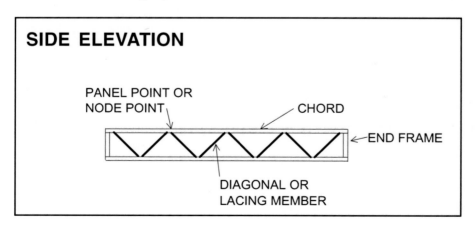

containers is that they are seldom what they appear to be - a 20 foot container is only 5.867m long internally which equates to 19' 3".

Transportation costs can be significant, be they associated with delivering the equipment from the manufacturer or during a tour. The efficient use of space within the container or lorry is therefore extremely important. With this in mind, industry standard trusses were soon established - for example, some trusses were 20.5 inches (521 mm) wide, so that four could be placed across the bed of a small truck.

A number of industry standard trusses have been developed over the years for various spans and load carrying characteristics. These trusses are known as Light Duty, Medium Duty, Heavy Duty and Par trusses within the range offered by Total Structures Inc and Total Fabrications Limited. Other manufacturers fabricate very similar trusses which are known by various names. For example, the General Purpose truss manufactured by James Thomas Engineering is very similar to the Medium Duty truss. These have been the work horses of the touring industry for many years. The chords are typically 50.8 mm (2 inches) in diameter to facilitate the attachment of equipment using clamps or scaffold clips which was seen as a prerequisite in the early years of the industry.

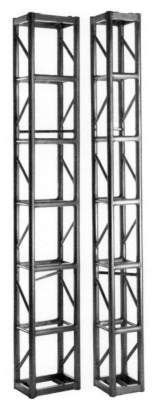

The Light Duty truss is 12 inches deep and either 18 or 12 inches wide. These trusses are used for applications where there is little headroom and the depth and bulk of the truss is critical. Because of their size, they do not have a high load carrying capacity and are not suitable for long spans. The deflection of these trusses under load can be quite high which is often not desirable. It will carry a uniformly distributed load of about 750 kg over a span of 10 metres.

The Medium Duty or General Purpose truss is 20.5 inches square. This is probably the most common size of truss which is manufactured. The truss is widely used throughout the industry

Light Duty Truss

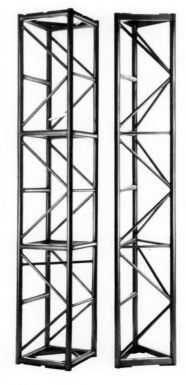

Medium Duty Truss   *Heavy Duty Truss*

especially for lighting grids supported from a main mother grid or from a roof structure. It has good load carrying characteristics and will carry a uniformly distributed load of about 1500 kg over a span of 10 metres.

The Heavy Duty truss is 20.5 inches wide and 30 inches deep. This truss is used where there is a requirement to carry heavy loads such as loudspeakers or similar equipment. In recent times the design has been changed so that the diagonals are 38 mm diameter tubes are used instead of the original 25mm diameter tubes. Other manufacturers have not changed the size of the diagonals on their version of this truss. You will recall that the size and steepness of the diagonals affects the shear capacity of the truss. A version of this truss is manufactured which is 30 inches wide for use with 18 inch towers in a ground support or roof structure. The 20.5 and 30 inch wide versions of this

Example of a Par truss

truss will carry a uniformly distributed load of about 2400 kg over a span of 10 metres.

The Par truss is 26 inches deep and either 15 or 30 inches wide - single hung or double hung. The trusses are generally offered in 8 or 10 foot lengths or their metric equivalent. These trusses are designed to carry the lighting fixtures within the body of the truss during transportation. The single hung trusses carry one lighting bar and a single row of lighting fixtures whereas the double hung version carries two rows of lighting fixtures. After the trusses are rigged, the lighting bars which support the fixtures are lowered so the fixtures protrude below the bottom of the truss. This can save time at the venue and can save transportation costs as less volume is taken up in transit as the lights do not have to travel separately.

The concept of a prerigged Par truss was then developed further by Total Structures Inc. to house moving lights, and this is now available for a number

Par truss carrying moving lights in transportation mode

Par truss carrying moving lights in performance mode

of different fixtures.

The cost of transportation was also addressed to some extent by considering trusses which could pack down into a smaller volume than when they were in use. The folding triangular truss was a good example of this. The truss comprises two ladder trusses, the top chords of which are joined

by hinges at regularly intervals along their length. The truss opens out into a triangle with the bottom chords being braced by a V brace. The truss has a high load capacity and can carry a uniformly distributed *Triangular Folding Truss* load of about 1900 kg over a span of 10 metres.

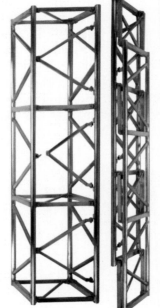

More recently, manufacturers have introduced innovative products and this has transformed the truss market virtually overnight. The Fold Flat Truss, as one might expect, folds flat laterally to about 25% of original width and has been in great demand since its launch because of it's space saving features for both transportation and storage. It has a high load carrying capacity for its size and is particularly liked as part of an outdoor roof structure. The roof for the Gloria Estafan concert mentioned at the beginning of this book uses this type of truss.

Fold Flat Truss

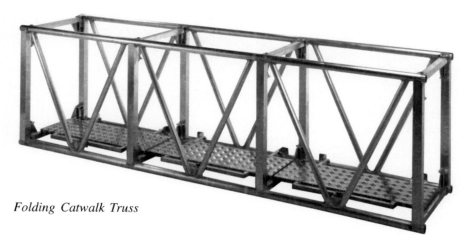

Folding Catwalk Truss

The Folding Catwalk Truss which uses the same basic concept as the Fold Flat truss but has an increased depth for greater load carrying capacity and for the inclusion of a walkway or crawl way.

As everyday shows became heavier and greater spans were required, manufacturers produced variants of the industry standard trusses. Total Fabrications Limited brought out the Serious range of trusses which use thick chord members and the turnbuckle connection. This range of trusses are of similar dimensions to the standard light, medium and heavy duty trusses but are not compatible with them because of the type of connection. They have a far greater load carrying capacity than their standard counterparts because of the much more efficient means of connection. The mother grid at Wembley Arena in London is constructed from Serious Medium and Heavy Duty trusses. It was installed in the autumn of 1997. The total payload of the grid is approximately 65 tonnes and so most shows can be accommodated. Other trusses have been developed recently – trusses for the exhibition market, walkway trusses where there are no internal members between the top chords so one can walk through without obstruction, custom high load capacity trusses etc.

So how were these trusses designed?

For a simply supported span of truss, with the loads acting vertically down, the chords carry the bending moment in a truss with the top chords in compression and the bottom chords in tension. The diagonals take the shear force in the truss. The steeper the diagonals, the greater the shear force the

Wembley Arena's 'Mother grid'

truss can withstand. We usually have diagonals at 45 degrees for a number of reasons, but where high shear forces need to be resisted, the angle of the diagonals to the chords is often increased to say 60 degrees. This shortens the length of the elements and aligns more closely with the direction of the shear force, thus making it more efficient.

It may be worth considering the design of a typical truss at this time. The design is governed by a number of factors. A truss as a whole is considered to consist of a number of pin ended struts. Each component of a truss needs to be considered individually as well as the truss as a whole.

The design of the principal components, the chords and the diagonals, is generally an iteration between the allowable compressive strength between the nodes which is governed by overall buckling of the member and the local squashing capacity of the member in the heat affected zone or the strength of the weld.

One would not expect to see chords or diagonals which appear to be very slender as the buckling capacity will be considerably less than the local squashing capacity. Conversely, one would not expect to see chords or diagonals which have a large diameter in relation to their length between nodes, as this would

Truss without diagonals

be structurally inefficient.

For example, medium duty trusses have 25.4 mm diameter diagonals which are about 700 mm long, whereas heavy duty truss has 38.1 mm diameter diagonals some 900 mm long.

However, just when it was all appearing to be relatively straightforward and comprehensible, let us consider the picture above.

Here we have a fairly large truss carrying loads above people's heads at an exhibition stand at a trade show in the Far East. You will note that the truss has no diagonals and as such has very little shear capacity.

I have seen many examples around the world of trusses being used on their sides - that is to say the diagonals are in the horizontal as opposed to the vertical plane. Quite how this is allowed to happen is difficult to understand - one has to question the competency of both the user and the inspection authorities.

Some manufacturers of aluminium truss do not weld all the way around a diagonal when it meets the chord. This is because it is quite difficult to undertake and can therefore be time consuming. They will tell you that it does not really matter and often think that the overall buckling of the diagonal in

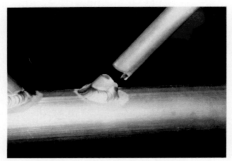

Example of failure of diagonal in tension

compression is more critical than local failure in the heat affected zone, even on short diagonals. This may be the case where the slender diagonals are used in deep trusses, in which case the buckling of the diagonals under load will be critical.

These photographs show a truss which has been load-tested to destruction. The diagonals were three quarters of an inch in diameter, 16 gauge material (1/16" or 1.6mm thick) and the chords were 2 inch 10 gauge (1/8" or 3.2mm thick). The diagonals were not welded all the way around.

The truss failed in shear due to the overstressing of the diagonals in compression in the heat affected zone where local buckling was observed and fracturing of the diagonals in tension in the heat affected zone. It is possible to see the 'necking' of the material at the zone of failure. This is a practical example of the discussions we had about Poisson's Ratio earlier.

It was clear that the strength of the diagonals at the point of failure was not totally mobilised as there was a gap between the unwelded part of the diagonal adjacent to the chord. Therefore, if the diagonal had been fully welded, then the truss would have failed at a greater applied load.

We can also just see the local squashing of the material in the heat affected zone where the strength of the metal has been reduced by welding. This is interesting in that it shows exactly the type of failure which is predicted in the British Standard 8118 The Structural Use of Aluminium.

The failure of this truss highlighted another problem. The diagonals were not aligned on the two vertical faces of the truss (see photograph on following page). That is to say that node on one chord did not line up with the node of the other top chord. Therefore, if a load is applied to the top of the truss, perpendicular to its length, it could be positioned at a node position on one chord but not on the other. We talked earlier about the fact that the loads should be applied to the truss at node position in order to reduce the risk of overstressing the chord due to the combination of axial and bending stresses. The top chord on one side of the truss appeared to have performed satisfactorily where the load was applied to the node whereas the other top chord was

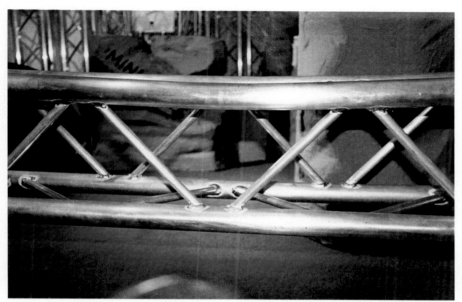

Nodes on the two chords do not line up, causing the truss to bend when a load is applied on top.

severely bent.

If the test loads had been located at the nodes and the diagonals had been welded all the way round, it is very likely that the failure loads would have been greater than those which caused failure to this sample.

Often, the way truss or tower modules are connected determines the strength, and therefore the load carrying capacity. A number of connection methods are used by manufacturers of truss. Some of these methods have been used in the manufacture of trusses and towers for many years before full engineering data was prepared. The various methods of connection each have advantages and disadvantages.

You will recall that the bending moment in a truss is carried by tension or compression in the chords and the shear force is carried by the diagonals. The purpose of a connection is to transfer the bending moment and shear force from one truss or tower module to the next, and the connections have to transfer these forces from one module to the next for the overall structure to be stable. Ideally, the connectors should not be the weak link in the construction of the truss as it is the connectors which are repeatedly used and are therefore subjected to wear and tear.

Quarter turn fasteners such as Camlocs are now being steadily phased out. The documentation that has recently been published by The Institution of Structural Engineers, the Health and Safety Executive and the British Standards Institute requires that fasteners have at least two actions to effect the connection. That is to say that quarter turn fasteners shall not be used, but connections which use nuts and bolts, shear pins and R clips and turnbuckles are permissible.

Fork end connections have been used in cranes, trains and other mechanical machines for many years. They are not, in my opinion, peculiar to the entertainment industry. The load is applied to the centre of the pin by the male fork end which is supported at each end by the female fork end. The pin is therefore in double shear. The allowable double shear for a pin is obviously double the value for single shear.

A fork end connection has to be attached to the chord in such a way to transfer both axial (tension or compression) and shear forces. The spigot part must penetrate the chord sufficiently to able to transfer the shear and be adequately attached to the chord to resist the axial forces. Similar principles apply for the turnbuckle connector. This is a structurally efficient as the axial force continues in line with the chords.

The method of connection using nuts and bolts is worth considering in detail. Firstly, we should consider how the forces are transferred.

You will now see the tortuous route which the forces have to take to join one

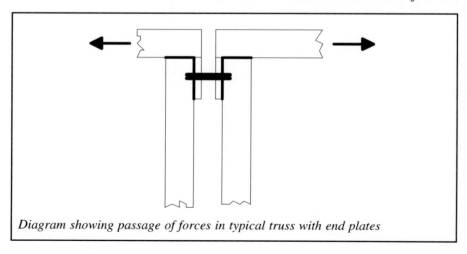

Diagram showing passage of forces in typical truss with end plates

truss to another by a simple nut and bolt : chord - weld - end frame - weld - plate - bolt - plate - weld - end frame - weld - chord.

This route is very similar to how the axial force in a chord of a tower is passed through to the next tower section as we cannot assume that the chords will bear against each other.

A number of checks have to be made in order to determine the strength of this type of connection.

Firstly, the allowable axial force in the bolt is ascertained. Next, the force which the plate can resist in bending without becoming overstressed is determined. Then the weld of the plate to the end frame is considered and finally the welding of the end frame to the chords. It is this last check which is often the most critical.

The allowable bending moment for each condition being considered is dependant on the distance between these conditions. If the chords are being considered, then the allowable bending moment depends on the allowable force in the chords and the vertical distance between them. If the bolts are being considered, then the allowable bending moment depends on the allowable force in the bolts and the distance between the bolts.

The allowable bending moment is then determined from the most critical factor. This is done by multiplying the force by the number of top or bottom chords by the distance apart. This only holds true for square or rectangular truss. The allowable bending moment for triangular trusses is determined in a slightly different way. The position of the neutral axis is determined and the allowable bending moment is the product of the force and the distance of the chord from the neutral axis.

Life gets more complicated when we start to consider what happens to a chord when adjacent diagonals are misnoded - that is to say when the centre lines of the members do not coincide at one point. If the diagonals are set up so that there are a series of "Vs" then the direction of force alternates for adjacent diagonals. One will be in tension, the next in compression, the next in tension and so on. For the force from one diagonal to get to the adjacent diagonal, the chord must bend.

This is demonstrated in the diagram overleaf. Bending stresses will develop which will reduce the allowable axial force in the chord. The capacity of the truss is therefore reduced accordingly.

The photograph on page 67 shows a truss which has been damaged and returned to the manufacturer for repair. Needless to say, the truss was

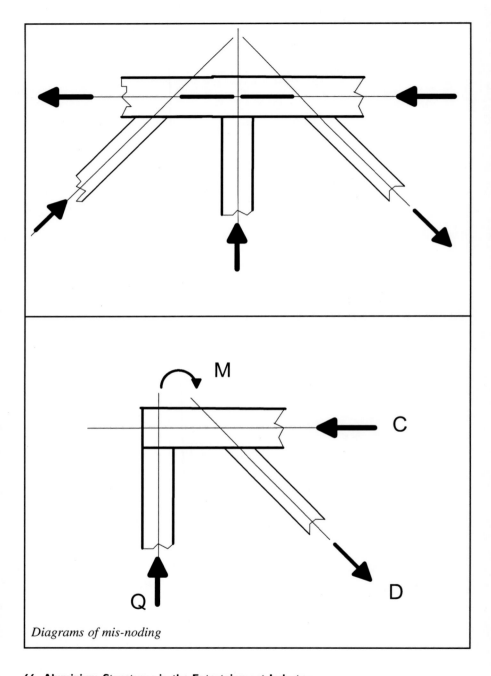

Diagrams of mis-noding

scrapped. However, it shows that the shear forces in the truss were very high and that the chords were bent by the forces in the diagonals due to the extent of misnoding.

The cause of the damage pictured below is uncertain, but it would appear that the tower has been subjected to a considerable bending moment and shear at the position of the sleeve due to lateral loads. This has resulted in unacceptably high forces in both the diagonals and the chords which has lead to permanent deformation of the elements of the tower.

A lot has been said about the flow of diagonals in trusses: "The 'V' should always point down"; "The 'V' should always point up"; "The diagonals should always alternate in direction". To understand these sweeping statements, one needs to appreciate how a truss is designed and the flow of forces between the chords and the diagonals.

Generally speaking, the diagonals in the most common trusses used in the entertainment industry are arranged in a series of 'V' shapes as in the 'Warren Truss'. The direction of force alternates between tension and compression. The direction of force in the diagonal depends where it is within the span and the distribution of load. The design of the diagonal should therefore account for both tension and compression. If the 'flow' is disrupted, and verticals are provided, then the direction of force in adjacent diagonals will be the same from the support position to the centre of the truss for the case of a uniformly distributed load as is the case in the 'Pratt Truss' or 'Howe Truss'.

Therefore, the direction or flow of the diagonals is not always critical. However, the user should check with the manufacturer.

12" tower with bent chords due to misnoding

When designing a truss or tower system, one usually tries to make the system structurally efficient. We try to make all the components 'fail' together, theoretically that is. Ideally, the allowable bending moment or shear force in a truss or the axial force in a tower due to one component should not be very much less than when another component is considered.

For example, it would not be preferable, in engineering terms, to have a truss where the end connections are so much stronger (or weaker) than the chords, or for the diagonals to be so slender that the allowable shear force is so much lower than would be required to utilise the bending strength of the truss. If the bending strength of the truss is such that it could safely carry 2000 kg over 10 metres, then the performance of the diagonals should be such that allowable shear force is approximately 1000kg.

This has certainly been the case for a number of the early designs of trusses used in the entertainment industry. For example, the strength of the weld between the main chords and the end frames of Medium Duty and Heavy Duty truss are considerably weaker than the chords themselves. The diagonals on early Heavy Duty trusses were only 1" (25.4 mm) in diameter. This resulted in a low shear strength as the diagonals were slender (comparatively long compared with their diameter or more properly, their radius of gyration). This was acknowledged when a full structural analysis of the truss was undertaken and the diagonals were subsequently changed to 1½" (38.1 mm diameter).

Other manufacturers have also appreciated that some early trusses were poorly designed in structural engineering terms. For example, James Thomas Engineering developed the "Supertruss" which utilised the full strength of the fork end connection by slotting the main chords to increase the length of the weld between the connector and the main chord itself.

Sometimes certain components could be very much smaller or thinner than would actually be required for the truss to perform satisfactorily. However, we have to consider the robustness of the component in a working environment. For example the engineering calculations may show that the diagonals of a certain truss may only need to be 1/16" (1.6mm) thick to resist the required shear loads. But the truss in question is to be used on a tour or is to be used by a rental company for their stock and therefore the truss must be robust and not susceptible to accidental damage. Hence, the thickness of the diagonals would be increased to say 1/8" (3.2mm).

Where trusses are to be used for exhibitions, for example, the user will normally treat the products with greater care as the appearance is more critical than for general use. Therefore, thinner gauge material may be considered if the strength of the truss remains adequate for the purpose.

The capacity of a truss in bending is largely dependant on the vertical distance between the chords. If the axial capacity of the chords is more critical than the method of connection, then the allowable bending moment is the product of the axial capacity of the chords and the centre line distance between those chords. Clearly, any reduction in the thickness of the chord will result in a reduction in the allowable bending moment.

If the truss is narrow, then it may buckle laterally when spanning larger distances. This is taken into account by reducing the allowable stress in the chords for larger spans. Therefore, the allowable bending moment is also reduced. Taking this to the extreme, a ladder truss would buckle sideways under load at spans where the compression in the top chord is greater than the allowable.

Generally speaking, the allowable payload on a box truss is governed by the

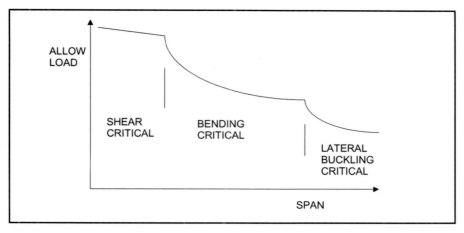

allowable shear force over short spans, bending capacity over medium spans and overall lateral buckling over long spans. An example of an allowable load chart where overall lateral buckling is critical would be thus:

We have talked about how bending in the chords affects the allowable tension or compression forces in the chords and how the application of load in the destruction testing of a truss caused distortion to one of the chords because the diagonals were not aligned. This can be taken a step further. If the truss is supported mid way between two nodes or a significant load is applied between two nodes then this could cause damage to the truss due to overstressing of the chord by high bending stresses. So a uniformly distributed load should also be applied as a series of point loads at node points. This applies to all trusses be they in a flown or ground supported rig or part of a roof structure.

A truss should also be supported at a node position as a support force can be considered as a large force applied in the opposite direction to the payload forces.

Often trusses which are 'flown' are supported on 'span sets' (round slings) which are wrapped around the top or the bottom chords of a truss. If this is the case then they should be rigged so that the truss is not subjected to lateral or vertical forces which would result in overstressing or damage to the chords or the truss as a whole.

For example, if the round sling is rigged so that the two parts of the round sling adjacent to the chain hook is at 45^0 to the vertical then the force in each part of the round sling is 70.71% of the support load. If this angle is increased to 60^0 to the vertical then the force in each part of the round sling is 100%

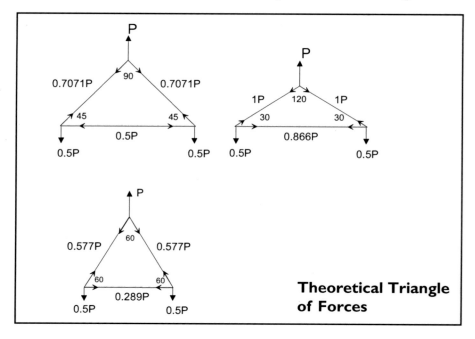

Theoretical Triangle of Forces

of the support load. More importantly, the compression force between the two attachment positions on the truss is 50% and 87% of the vertical load when the angles of the parts of the round sling are 45^0 and 60^0 to the vertical respectively. It is this compression load between the corresponding points on the chords which may damage the truss.

If the round sling is used so that it is choked then the forces are different again and depend upon the angle of the various sections of the round sling to the vertical. It can be seen that the rigging of the truss can be achieved in a number of ways all of which have differing effects on the truss. Therefore, it is recommended that the user obtain advice from the manufacturer of the round slings, a rigger or other competent person with experience in these matters.

Span sets, round slings and some other rigging accessories are made of polyester. These could melt in the event of fire. If they are often the primary means of support, then users often consider providing a secondary 'safety' in the form of steel wire ropes, chains or other mechanical means of support. This notion stemmed from a requirement from the Greater London Council that steel wire rope secondary 'safeties' should be used when shows were staged at Wembley Arena. The explanation apparently was that the trusses should be secure and not collapse as they could injure firemen who were fighting a fire in a building which may be filled with smoke.

However, this practice of using steel wire rope 'safeties' could be flawed. Indeed, OSHA in America state the operating limits for various types of slings and chain. They are as follows:

CFR 1910 General Industry Orders (OSHA)

1910.184(e) Alloy steel chain slings

(6)   Safe operating temperatures. Alloy steel chain slings shall be permanently removed from service if they are heated above $1000\,^0$F. When exposed to service temperatures in excess of $600\,^0$F, maximum working load limits permitted in Table N-184-1 shall be reduced in accordance with the chain or sling manufacturer's recommendations.

1910.184(f) Wire rope slings

(3)   Safe operating temperatures. Fibre core wire rope slings of all grades shall be permanently removed from service if they are exposed to temperatures in excess of $200\,^0$F. When non fibre core wire rope slings of any grade are used at temperatures above $400\,^0$F or below

minus 60 °F, recommendations of the sling manufacturer regarding use at that temperature shall be followed.

1910.184(h) Natural and synthetic fibre rope slings

(2)   Safe operating temperatures. Natural and synthetic fibre rope slings, except for wet frozen slings, may be used in a temperature range from minus 20 °F to plus 180 °F without decreasing the working load limit. For operations outside this temperature range and for wet frozen slings, the sling manufacturer's recommendations shall be followed.

In summary, in America, synthetic round slings or span sets, steel wire ropes and chains are permissible in environments where the temperature does not exceed 180 °F, 400 °F and 600 °F respectively (82 °C, 204 °C and 315 °C). Clearly, these figures are not consistent with those experienced in a fire. Indeed, there was an instance where a fire took place in a theatre in America. The fire lasted between 10 and 15 minutes before it was extinguished by the sprinkler system. During that time a number of steel wire rope assemblies melted and the scenery collapsed.

However, it is worth noting (from above) that aluminium reduces it strength by 15%, 45% and 85% when the temperature is raised to 100, 200 and 300 degrees centigrade respectively. It can therefore be seen that the possibility that the synthetic round sling or steel wire rope may melt in the event of fire may be only part of a larger issue - the aluminium truss structure may collapse due to loss of strength of the parent material Venue owners should therefore consider advising the fire brigade of the dangers of walking under structures during a major fire.

The use of span sets and round slings is widespread in the industry. They are simple to use, but some basic principles should be observed. For example, if the truss is to be hung from the top, then the loads should be applied to the bottom of the truss for it to remain stable and reduce the tendency to twist. If the truss is supported by the bottom chords and the loads are applied to the top chords, then the truss has a tendency to rotate. In essence, they should be used with care and thought of where the forces will be resisted. For example, they should not be used to support load between node points because vertical and/or horizontal bending of the chord may result in local over-stressing. They must always be used by a competent person with adequate experience.

Factors of safety for chain, wire rope, round slings and the like are outside the scope of this book. However, there are requirements that figures of 5 or 6 and sometimes as high as 10 be adopted. One could argue that these figures are excessive, especially if equipment is checked and inspected on a regular basis. However, the user may become complacent and even overload certain items in the knowledge that there is some spare capacity before failure.

5 DESIGN STANDARDS

Methods of analysing materials used in construction have changed in recent times. The old approach, which is still in use in the UK and America for some materials, establishes allowable stress for tension, compression, shear, bearing, etc., based upon specified material properties. These allowable stresses are typically based on minimum 'factors of safety' of 1.65 against yield stress and 1.95 against fracture or buckling. This approach to engineering design which employs explicit 'factors of safety' is called Allowable Stress Design (ASD).

You should note that none of the factors of safety in ASD is against 'failure' of a structure as a whole. The greater the consequences, the larger the 'factor of safety'. If material in a structure yields in service, the structure has been permanently deformed and will require repair or replacement. However, if the material fractures or buckles in service, catastrophic failure may result. Consequently, the factor of safety against fracture stress is greater than against yield stress.

The more modern, reliability derived approach which looks at the resistance of the structure and ensures that it is greater than the factored load effects, is referred to as Load and Resistance Factor Design (LRFD). The Aluminium Association in America allows both ASD and LRFD approaches to design, and so does the American Institute of Steel Construction with respect to steel structure design, but the intent of both organisations is to eliminate completely the ASD approach with its explicit factors of safety. The American Concrete Institute has done this for reinforced concrete design: it is now all LRFD.

In the UK, BS 8118 'The Structural Use of Aluminium' employs solely an LRFD approach. The standard which was previously used, CP 118, uses the ASD approach. CP 118 is now considered to be obsolete.

BS 8118 is a comprehensive and complex document. The consideration of weld effects is extensive and much more involved than the approach taken in CP 118, and it is considered to be much more realistic. For example, the extent of the heat affected zone is dependant on the material thickness in BS 8118, whereas CP 118 considers the distance to be 25.4mm (1 inch) whatever the thickness of the connecting plys. This simplistic approach is also used in the

Specification for Aluminum Structures published by the Aluminum Association in America.

The story of other standards is very similar to that in America in that the standard for reinforced concrete in the UK uses an LRFD approach as do the steel and timber standards. However, an ASD version of the UK steel design standard remains in use due to pressure from 'establishment engineers' who do not want to change their design approach.

In Germany, the Deutsches Institut Fur Normung DIN 4113 'Aluminium Construction Under Predominantly Static Loading; Static Analysis and Structural Design' uses an ASD approach.

There has been some discussion and indeed action about harmonising the Codes of Practice and Standards within Europe. I have discussed the issue of a European aluminium code with British Standards Institute, and they indicated that there has not been agreement about the base document for the Standard although BS 8118 would appear to be the preferred base document by many, the Germans and the French have objected. Their feeling was that there was not likely to be a European aluminium standard until at least 2010.

Two important documents have recently been published by the British Standards Institute: BS 7905, Part 2 Specification for the Design and Manufacture of Aluminium and Steel Trusses and Towers, and BS 7906, Part 2 Code of Practice for the Use of Aluminium and Steel Trusses and Towers (available from BSI Customer Services on +44 208 996 9001).

These could have a profound effect on the entertainment industry as we strive to be more credible in the eyes of statutory authorities and to place a greater emphasis on safety, accountability, and professionalism. They deal with the basic building blocks of concert touring lighting grids, ground support systems, and outdoor structures and are the first standards issued written specifically on the subject anywhere in the world. I will now explain why the Standards were written, what they contain, and how they should be implemented.

In the early days of concert touring, trusses were often fabricated and used without allowable load tables or certification. As show equipment became heavier, the authorities became aware of the dangers involved and demanded that the user substantiate the use of trusses by calculation or testing. Major manufacturers provided structural calculations or test results and allowable load tables for the standard products. In the UK, these were based on CP 118, The Structural Use of Aluminium, which was superseded by BS 8118 in the early 1990s. AA SAS30, Specifications for Aluminum Structures, now superseded by AA ADM1, was used by engineers in the United States.

Structural engineers soon realised that these concert touring structures were used repetitively and in different configurations in potentially dangerous situations, and that the simple application of these existing standards might not be adequate – particularly considering society's expectations.

The design, manufacture, and use of aluminium trusses and towers in the entertainment industry was thus deemed to be a very important issue. The writing of a suitable standard was one of the first projects undertaken by Entertainment Services and Technology Association's Technical Standards Program. Within the Technical Standards Program, the Rigging Working Group is responsible for the writing of a number of standards ranging from the construction of wire rope ladders through manual counterweight systems to flying performers. The standard was written and revised through the public review process, and approved by the Technical Standards Committee and the ESTA Board. The standard was then submitted to ANSI and has now become a full American Standard, ANSI E1.2 'Design, manufacture and use of aluminum trusses and towers'.

However, a number of major manufacturers have fabrication facilities both in America and the UK, and many shows start in the UK and then tour the US and vice versa. Thus, the need for a parallel document in the UK was obvious. BS 7905, Part 2 and BS 7906, Part 2 taken together are that parallel document.

It is often difficult and sometimes impossible to formally draft parallel standards with other bodies. Often, the simplest way to have compatible national standards of different nations is to have the same person or persons sit on the two different national committees, and that is what has been done in this case. I was that person. It has been the Rigging Working Group's intention to have the ESTA and ANSI standards as close as possible with other national standards elsewhere in the world and with international standards. It was also recognised that it is in the Rigging Working Group's interest to help other standards bodies draft standards that are consistent with the ESTA and ANSI standards.

The documents are very similar, but not identical. The British documents have had the Americanism's removed and references to ANSI standards removed and replaced with analogous British Standards. Steel trusses and towers in the UK are not uncommon and hence the standard was developed further to include the use of this material. The draft was then submitted to BSI through committee MHE/3/13 who have been writing a British Standard on lifting equipment for performance, broadcast and similar applications. BSI have a slightly different format for their standards in that design and manufacture should be dealt with in a specification and use should be covered in a separate code of practice, so the standard was then redrafted into two separate documents. After some discussion, the documents went to public review, comments were returned, and the text was updated. The British Standard was published before the American document on which it is based, and its existence is now being publicised throughout the industry and local authorities in the UK.

The specification, BS 7905, Part 2, covers engineering, design, analysis, and documentation which must be available from the manufacturer. In engineering a structure, BS 8118 covers the main design issues. However, the rigours of touring needed to be accounted for. Much discussion took place between the structural engineers in ESTA's Rigging Work Group and a load reduction factor of 0.85 to cover wear and tear was agreed upon. This means that the design load for a given span is multiplied by 0.85 to give the allowable static equivalent load.

One particularly useful part of the standard is the definition of the minimum amount of information that shall be produced for the end user regarding care and use. This information is supplied by the manufacturer to assist the user and includes load tables and charts showing allowable loads for a variety of load configurations and the anticipated associated deflections and also information regarding handling, transportation, erection and inspection.

Included in this information is the matter of factors of safety. Much has been made of these by a number of manufacturers and users often ask about this. The standard now requires that if the manufacturer makes a statement about factors of safety in the information he publishes, then he shall state to what condition the design refers. That is to say if the factor of safety is against overstressing, ultimate failure, excessive deflection, or whatever.

The code of practice, BS 7906, Part 2, deals primarily with the use and inspection of the equipment. Not surprisingly, the standard requires that the user complies with the guidelines and recommendations set out by the manufacturer. It also requires the user to fully consider the loads which are applied to the structure, including light and sound equipment and multicore cables on one hand and wind, rain, and snow on the other. Loads induced on structures from fall arrest systems should also be considered.

Users often ask for the manufacturer to specify the design life of truss modules. This is very difficult to assess and depends on a variety of things such as the number of uses, the frequency of use, the amount of load be applied on each use, and how the trusses are handled and transported. The standard sets out basic requirements for handling. These should be adhered to as a minimum and surpassed wherever possible to prolong the life of the equipment.

The standard requires detailed drawings and calculations be prepared for each time the structure is used and that it is assembled in accordance with those drawings. This cannot be seen as an onerous requirement as adequate drawings would be necessary to enable the structure to be assembled correctly and subsequently checked.

Inspections are frequently overlooked by rental and production companies. It is not now, and never has been, acceptable to continue to use truss and tower modules without regular and appropriate inspections, but this requirement is now clearly written into the standard. The inspections are split into two categories: frequent and periodic. The frequent inspections are intended to be undertaken each time the elements are used, whereas the periodic inspections are much more onerous and would normally be carried out once per year, depending on frequency and mode of use. These inspections would be more rigorous for equipment that lifts people, such as flying performers. The periodic inspections are further split to cover stationary and moving installations.

The standard indicates that a full list of inspection procedures is beyond the scope of the document. The procedures for a large complex structure are more involved than for something simpler and therefore the lists shown in the standard should been seen as a minimum. LOLER (the Lifting Operations and Lifting Equipment Regulations 1998) requires that the inspection procedures are defined by a qualified person. However, although LOLER states that the inspections are statutory and defines the period between inspections, it does allow these periods to be modified by a qualified person. For example, the structural engineer may deem that certain critical elements of a moving structure be inspected thoroughly every month or perhaps before every move. The suggested inspection procedures enable the user to determine when a truss module should be taken out of service. The standard states that the assessment of any damage and any repairs required should be undertaken by a qualified person.

But who does these inspections? The regular inspections are essentially visual and should be done by a competent person: someone who has experience in the use of truss structures and knows what to look for. Most experienced riggers would be capable of fulfilling this task. The periodic inspections are much more thorough and require that records are signed and kept. These inspections shall be carried out by a qualified person such as a chartered engineer. It should be noted that the owner of lifting equipment now has a legal obligation to inspect such equipment every six months under the requirements of LOLER.

In summary, these standards serve a number of purposes. They demand that the manufacturer conducts his business in a professional manner. They set out the information which the user shall expect from the manufacturer. They require the user to employ competent persons, to operate the equipment correctly and to undertake inspections on a regular basis. The flip side, of course, is that the authorities now have a bench mark from which to assess the design and use of trusses and towers in the entertainment industry. We should all now be aware of our responsibilities for the safe use of equipment. "It will be all right" is no longer acceptable. "We didn't know" can no longer be an excuse. "You should have told me" is no longer valid. On who's head be it now?

A certain amount of standard writing has been and is currently being undertaken in America and Britain by people within the entertainment industry. The intention is to have these standards published and adopt them as national standards which could be used in countries which do not have such documents.

There is a danger that if we do not write these standards, then they will be written by others who have very little knowledge or experience of the entertainment industry – which could have far reaching effects. We might have to comply with impractical, unworkable and misinformed standards or other documents

This has already happened. When the Institution of Structural Engineers published a revised version of "Temporary Demountable Structures" in October 1995, without any consultation with the entertainment industry, it caused so much adverse comment that it is has been substantially rewritten. I was heavily involved with the rewriting of this document in late 1997 and 1998. It was published in March 1999 and is now widely used and is accepted by the industry as a standard document in the UK.

'The Guide to Health, Safety and Welfare at Pop Concerts and Similar Events' was published by the Health and Safety Executive in 1993. It was substantially rewritten and was published in October 1999 with the new title of 'The Event Safety Guide'. The section regarding structures indicates that reference should be made to 'Temporary Demountable Structures' and does not offer specific information on structural design or inspection and so conflicting guidance has, for the most part, been eradicated.

6 FACTORS OF SAFETY

'Factors of Safety' were the subject of much debate during the drafting of the ANSI E1.2, Entertainment Technology – Design, Manufacture and Use of Aluminum Trusses and Towers standard and it would be appropriate to discuss these here.

The factor safety of a structure is a measure of the reliability of that structure. The factor of safety can therefore be defined as the ratio between the load which will cause failure of the structure and the allowable load applied to the structure as defined in the load charts or structural calculations.

It could also be considered as the ratio between the bending moment which would cause failure and the maximum bending moment due to the applied loads. A similar definition could be determined for shear forces.

Unlike some manufacturers, my company does not advertise the factor of safety for which our structures are designed. There are a number of very good reasons why not. Firstly, why do customers need to know the failure load? All they really need to know is the allowable loads on the truss or structure. If they know that the allowable load is say 1000 kg and the factor of safety is say 3:1 against failure then they may be tempted to load the truss with 1250, 1500, 2000 kg or even more which would overstress or permanently damage some elements of the truss. This could be extremely dangerous especially when you bear in mind that elements of modern buildings often have a 'factor of safety' against yield and fracture or buckling of about 1.6 and 2.0 respectively.

This definition of a factor of safety requires that we know the failure load of and the applied load on a structure. The allowable load should be easily determined, but the failure load is not.

For example, say we fabricate 100 aluminium trusses, as identical as we can make them. We test them to failure with a central point load, but we only conduct one test per truss because we wreck the trusses in testing. Our 100 tests give us varied results, but we have lots of test data so we can establish the mean, median, maximum and minimum failure loads.

We ask a statistician to use our data and tell us what load is 100% certain not to cause failure of any truss - ever. He calculates this load to be zero.

'Ever' is too limiting and is not very helpful. We search for some better definition of 'failure load' using our data. He calculates the load that has a probability of one in one thousand of causing our trusses to fail. We decide that this is a good definition of failure load. However, we hope to manufacture 1000 trusses and we do not want any of them to fail, so we need more reliability. We collect more data, and do some more statistical analysis, and we find the load which has an acceptably low probability - one in five million - of resulting in failure. We define this as the 'permissible service load'. Now we can define the 'factor of safety' as the 1 in 1000 failure load divided by the 1 in 5 million permissible service load. After all this, we may find the 'factor of safety' is something like 1:5.

Now suppose an enterprising customer conducts a failure test with a particular load configuration on one of our trusses, and finds that it fails at a load 2.62 times the permissible service load. He concludes that the 'factor of safety' is 2.62. Now what do we do? We have used basically the same definition of 'factor of safety', but we have two very different answers.

What we are really trying to do is to design trusses that meet some minimum criterion for reliability, and there are other methods and other notions of 'factor of safety' to help us do this. Among the main aids are well developed design standards such as the British Standard 8118 The Structural Use of Aluminium and the "Specifications for Aluminum Structures" from the Aluminium Association in America. These documents provide us with the means of establishing the resistance of the constituent parts of the truss, such as the chords, the diagonals, the welds, and other parts, to various loads, including tension, compression and shear. As a consequence of the variability of the resistance, these are reduced by a multiplier for various load conditions and design the trusses so that the load conditions do not produce load effects in the components that exceeded the factored resistance. Since there is inevitably some variability in the applied loads, the standards provide us with factors greater than one to apply to the design loads. These load factors vary depending upon the type of load and its variability. The effects of the factored loads must be less than the reduced resistance of the truss components. All this is aimed at the same result that we were attempting to accomplish with our hypothetical example, i.e. reducing the probability of failure to below some acceptably low level.

The ESTA rigging task group that drafted the ANSI E1.2 standard had significant discussion about appropriate factors of safety. Since the British

Standard and the Aluminium Association standards already existed and are based on years of research, testing and experience with aluminium structures, it was appropriate to use it as the primary reference standard. When all was discussed and considered, the only real difference between many of the entertainment applications of aluminium truss structures and those for which the aluminium standards were clearly written to address is that, in entertainment, structures are often made of modules which have been used repeatedly to build many structures for many shows. Even with regular inspection, it is likely that repetitive use will increase the variability of the resistance to loads of these components. Consequently, the reliability of structures employing pieces in repetitive use would be potentially less than intended in the British and American standards.

This concern was addressed by reducing the design strength or resistance of trussing intended for repetitive use. A minimum reduction factor of 0.85 is included in the standard. For entertainment structures that are not comprised of modules in repetitive use, the requirements of the existing standards are deemed to be adequate.

The normal design standards are generally used for aluminium structures in permanent installations. These standards are deemed to be quite adequate for the purpose. After all, the philosophy behind the writing of BS 8118 The Structural Use of Aluminium is very similar to (say) the British Standard for the structural use of steel or concrete which are generally used by structural engineers in the design of new buildings. These aluminium structures should be subjected to the inspection regime discussed later.

What about variability of loads? In many respects, the loads to which entertainment structures are subject are easily quantifiable. Large variability exists in loads from wind or human occupancy, so this needs to be determined conservatively. Building codes exist for this purpose. The maximum loads to which the structure is to be subjected must be predictable. No 'factor of safety' can adequately compensate for not anticipating the maximum loads on a structure.

We should also consider actions that can erode the factor of safety.

Aluminum truss is frequently powder coated black to go out on tour. Then it rattles around in the trucks, is manhandled in and out of venues, is dragged across the floor, generally abused, and then it returns to the rental house scratched and scraped. So, how does the rental house make good the damaged paint for the next tour? "Shot blast it and send it back to the powder coaters" is the easy answer. No, it is not so easy!

This scenario recently has been the subject of much discussion within the Rigging Working Group of ESTA's Technical Standards Program. Repeated powder coating and abrasion blasting can affect the strength of aluminum trusses used in the entertainment industry, so revisions to ANSI E1.2 Design, Manufacture and Use of Aluminum Trusses and Towers are deemed to be necessary, and the process of revising that standard has been started.

To understand how repeated powder-coating can affect aluminum trusses, it helps to first consider the aluminum itself. There are a very large number of different types of aluminum alloy currently available in the United States and the rest of the world. Each alloy has pre-determined strength characteristics and minimum tensile, compression and shear specifications that are found in the Aluminum Association and ASTM documents. However, the most common aluminum alloy used in the entertainment industry in the U.S. is 6061-T6.

The "6061" is a description of the chemical composition of the alloy and "T6" indicates a specific sequence of treatments that the material underwent after it was extruded. Often more digits follow the T6 designation to indicate a variation in the treatment, and that variation can significantly alter the characteristics of the material with respect to the original T temper. These digits often relate to one of the following:

- The solution used for heat-treatment or precipitation treatment
- The amount of cold work after the solution heat-treatment
- The stress-relieving treatment

For example, 6061-T651 is 6061 alloy in the T6 temper that has been solution heat-treated, stress-relieved by stretching a controlled amount, and then artificially aged. This artificial aging is typically done by heating the material to 360°F for 8 hours. At this time the metal has typically reached its peak strength and lowest ductility. That is, it has now been made as strong and as least likely to permanently stretch as possible. Aging needs to be stopped at this point. The aging process slows down with increased heating time, but once the peak strength has been reached, a number of hours at this elevated temperature will make the material start to soften, becoming more ductile and losing strength. However, the changes due to additional aging are gradual. For example, a couple of additional hours of exposure at 380°F after the T6 temper has been reached would not alter the strength very significantly, but a longer period at this or at a higher temperature certainly would.

What significance does all this have to powder coating of truss?

Typically, the powder coating process involves heating the truss to 380°F for 20 minutes. The strength is not significantly affected if the material is heated to 380°F for about 2 hours after the T6 temper has been achieved, but after that time further heating may reduce the strength. Therefore, heating the truss five times after fabrication is about as often as this can be done without risking significantly affecting the strength of the truss. Therefore, the first draft of the proposed revisions to the ANSI E1.2 standard includes the statements:

"The application of powder coating shall use only a low cure process. The heating of truss and tower modules shall only be done in accordance with section 6.3 of the Aluminum Association "Specification and Guidelines for Aluminum Structures." and: "Repetitive coating using a heat process shall be limited to a maximum of 5 applications per truss/tower module. At no time during those applications shall the module be subjected to a temperature in excess of 193^0C (380^0F) for longer than 30 minutes."

The effects of heating are cumulative, so, clearly, keeping records to show the powder coating history is essential to ensure that the truss is not inadvertently heated often enough or long enough to reduce the strength of the material. Hence, the proposed revisions state:

"Records shall be kept detailing the application of any coating or surface finish with particular detail regarding processes requiring the application of heat".

But what about other truss materials? After all, much of the truss fabricated in Europe uses 6082-T6 aluminum alloy, and ANSI E1.2 does not preclude the use of other aluminum alloys. Other alloys and thermal-mechanical processing routes may be affected by heating somewhat differently, but the guidance offered in the proposed revisions to ANSI E1.2 is still fundamentally good. A truss manufacturer could develop more specific recommendations for the company's products by examining samples of the metal subjected to elevated temperatures for different periods of time to document the changes in strength and ductility. This is not hard for a manufacturing firm, but it is not something you can do easily at home!

It should be noted that mild steel is not affected in the same way as aluminum is at these temperatures. Steel truss is used in the U.S. mainly in custom scenery construction and is not seen a lot on tour, but it could be powder coated repeatedly without affecting its strength.

Applying conventional solvent-based paints usually does not involve heating the truss, so heat affects should not be an issue, but a prospective truss-painter should still do some research to see if there are any possible corrosive effects on the aluminum. Therefore, the proposed revision to the standard includes a clause saying:

"Consideration shall be given to any coating or surface finishing techniques used in manufacturing that may affect the structural properties and load bearing capabilities of the truss or tower sections."

Generally speaking, it would be prudent to touch-up damaged paintwork spots rather than opt to repaint the truss entirely. However, if a truss is so badly scratched that repainting is necessary, then we need to consider how to remove the paint without removing or weakening the aluminum. Abrasion blasting (also known as "sand blasting") is a common paint-removal process, but the Aluminum Association Specifications are very clear about this process. Clause 6.7 states "Abrasion blasting shall not be used on aluminum less than or equal to 1/8 in. (3mm) thick." Does this affect the entertainment industry? Very much so. The vast majority of truss and tower includes chords, diagonals and secondary members that are 1/8" thick. The clause therefore effectively prohibits the use of "sand blasting" of the majority of trusses. The proposed changes to the standard reflect this:

"Abrasion-blasting shall not be used on aluminum less than or equal to 1/8 inch (3mm) thick, in accordance with section 6.7 of the Aluminum Association 'Specification and Guidelines for Aluminum Structures.'"

So how do we remove any paint prior to re-powder coating or re-painting? Answer: very carefully! Aluminum has good corrosion resistance due to the protective oxide film that forms on the surface upon contact with air. However, it is susceptible to corrosion if subjected to strong acid or alkaline environments. Then the oxide layer may become soluble and surface discoloration and roughening will occur with white powdery residues being formed. This can be seen if truss is left outdoors in industrial or seaside locations for protracted periods; then, surface pitting and white powdery oxides are frequently observed.

Therefore, the use of paint strippers or etching prior to powder coating needs to carefully considered. Clearly, certain solvents can be very corrosive and detrimental to aluminum and hence research should be carried prior to their use. Section 6.7 of the Aluminum Association Standards quite candidly suggests:

"Exposed metal surfaces shall be cleaned with a suitable chemical cleaner such as a solution of phosphoric acid and organic solvents meeting United

States Military Specification MIL-M-10578."

The proposed revisions to the ANSI E1.2 standard address the issue a little differently by stating:

"Removal of coatings and surface finishes if done with chemicals shall be carried out only after consulting with the chemical manufacturer to insure the chemical will not affect the mechanical properties of the aluminum."

It should be noted that it is also important to remove all the paint remover or cleaner – not only from the outside of the truss but also from the inside. Pressure relief holes are frequently drilled in diagonals and secondary members prior to welding. If the truss is dipped in chemicals to remove grease and dirt prior to anodizing or powder coating, then great care must be taken to ensure that all the chemicals are flushed out and no chemicals are left inside the members.

Many companies want to have the truss looking like new at the start of a tour, but achieving this has to be done with care. Powder coats and paints need to be applied and removed in such a way that the truss maintains its strength. Failure do so may leave the truss all dressed up but with nowhere to go.

7 ASSESSMENT OF LOADS

The manufacturer and/or designer of a structural system requires a certain amount of information before he (or she) can offer a workable solution.
Below is a list of such information:

TYPICAL CHECK LIST
INFORMATION REQUIRED BY MANUFACTURER

Truss
Span
Any Depth Restrictions for Truss Sections
Static Payload
Dynamic Loads
Temporary or Permanent
Means of Suspension
Number of Suspension Points
Geographical Location

Indoor Grid
Drawing of Grid
Any Depth Restrictions for Truss Sections
Height of Towers (if applicable)
Static Payload
Dynamic Loads
Temporary or Permanent
Means of Suspension
Number of Suspension Points
Geographical Location

Outdoor Grid
Design Wind Speed
Drawing of Grid
Height of Towers

Static Payload
Dynamic Loads
Temporary or Permanent
Windage Area of Equipment to be Used
Ground Conditions
Location of Existing Overhead and Underground Services
Geographical Location

Outdoor Roof
Design Wind Speed
Drawing of Roof
Height of Towers
Trim Height Required
Static Payload
Dynamic Loads
Temporary or Permanent
Windage Area of Equipment to be Used
Side and Back Walls Required
Ground Conditions
Location of Existing Overhead and Underground Sservices
Geographical Location

The incorrect assessment of loads is potentially one of the most common reasons for structural failure.

Let us explore this statement in more detail and consider the repercussions of not assessing the applied loads correctly.

The load which a single truss, lighting rig, ground support or roof structure is required to support can be split into three main categories - dead and live static loads, dynamic loads and wind loads. Each of these types of load can and should be assessed for every application. The assessment and subsequent analysis should be carried out by a competent person.

The payload is sometimes known as the 'superimposed' load or 'live' load. 'Dead' load is the self-weight of the truss or structure being considered. A 'dynamic' load is a load which moves or vibrates.

The weights of lighting fixtures, sound equipment, cables, trusses and motors (and chain) are generally available form the respective manufacturers. An allowance should also be made for rigging hardware and accessories.

Particular care should be taken when considering the loads from cable drops which can be substantial. When the truss or lighting rig is near to the ground, the load from the cable drop will be relatively small. However, the load will increase linearly as the structure is raised.

Human occupancy cannot be so easily determined. However, the building codes do suggest the weight of a standard person. Typical British Standards suggest that a person should be assumed to weigh 0.9 kN (91 kg or about 200lbs)

The allowable static payloads for various load configurations and spans are generally provided by truss manufacturers in the form of load charts which we discussed earlier.

The static payload is defined as the static equivalent loading imposed upon a static structure. This must include the weight of the luminaires, associated equipment, any rigging trusses and their fixings, fastenings and hoisting equipment, together with the electrical cables.

If the truss is moved when the payload is in place, the payload is considered to have a greater weight for design purposes. This increase in weight is determined by what is known as the 'dynamic magnification factor' and this factor is always greater than one. The application of this factor effectively reduces the load which can be applied to a truss which moves.

The actual payload multiplied by the 'dynamic magnification factor' will give the static equivalent load. The value of the 'dynamic magnification factor' depends on the motor and the type of motor controller and should be determined by the user.

Soft start motor controllers and computer driven motor controllers have been developed which start the motor at a slow speed before ramping up to normal operating speed. The use of such controllers will undoubtedly reduce the 'dynamic magnification factor'.

The loads imposed on structures from fall arrest equipment in the event of a person falling need to be explored in great detail. Comment on the forces imposed on the body by the fall arrest equipment is outside the scope of this book.

How does this affect the truss and what loads are applied to the truss?

Fall arrest equipment is a very important development in the safety of riggers and other personnel working at height in the entertainment industry. In recent years a number of people have been killed or seriously injured around the world after falling from height. The mandatory use and widespread adoption of fall arrest equipment is long overdue. However, extreme caution should be exercised when securing these systems to a truss grid structure or an existing building and a full under-standing of the restraining forces and their associated load paths is essential as your life may depend on it.

Imagine the scene where a person clips onto the horizontal safety line which is attached to the truss in some way. He walks along the truss to go and focus some lights or get to his followspot chair. Mid way along the truss from the wire rope ladder he slips and falls, the horizontal line deflects in order to arrest his fall and the tension in the line increases dramatically.

The increase in tension in the line is dependant on whether shock absorbers have been fitted to the horizontal line and the lanyard, the length of the wire and how far the person is allowed to fall. Typical values for a 100 kg (0.98 kN) weight falling two metres from a line 18 metres (60 ft) long would be between 1 and 2 tonnes (9.81 and 19.62 kN) depending on whether shock absorbers are fitted. If the person is carrying equipment when he falls or there are two people attached, then the load in the horizontal line will be even greater.

But where do these forces go? They must be resisted by something. There are three main options - the truss, the motors which support the truss, or the existing building.

In this example, the 'catenary wire' takes the form of a steel wire rope

Example of catenary wires between motors

although webbing straps are often used. The wire is attached to the shackle below the motor. In the event of a fall, the load in the catenary wire would try to pull the motors together. This would be resisted by the truss below which would be subjected to high compression forces for which it has probably not been designed.

A number of types of fall arrest systems are simply attached to the truss. But is this really wise? What do we need to consider? We need to establish the magnitude of the loads applied to the truss and how these could possibly affect the truss.

Some systems are simply attached to the top chords of a truss by way of two frames and the line is tensioned. It is known that application of loads between the node points may lead to local bending of the members which could lead to damage to or failure of the truss. It is critical to consider how these frames are attached to the chords of the truss and the local effects on the chords which could affect the ability of the truss to sustain other loads.

For the configuration of the support frame shown above, the vertical forces in the connections are considerable. We should consider the effects of these forces in detail.

If we assume that the force F is 1000 kg, the distance between the node or panel points of the truss is say 1000 mm and the connection of the frame is mid way between panel points, then the bending moment in the tube due to the vertical force is 0.5 x 1000 x 1.0 / 4 = 125 kgm (approx. 1.23 kNm). If the chord of the truss is 50.8 mm x 3.2 mm circular tube, then the bending stress in the chord is $1.23 \times 10^6 / 4277 = 287$ N/mm^2. The axial stress is 0.5 x 1000 x 9.81 / 479 = 10.24 N/mm^2. These are both working stresses, that is to say they are the actual stresses without any design factors being applied.

The maximum bending or overall stress, P_0 for 6082 -T6 aluminium alloy stated in BS 8118 The Structural Use of Aluminium is 255 N/mm^2. But this is a factored stress and the allowable working stress is therefore about 255 / 1.2

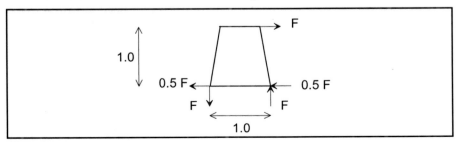

x 1.33 = 160 N/mm². The alloy commonly used in the US is 6061-T6 which has slightly less favourable properties.

We can therefore conclude that if the frames are attached mid way between node or panel points and the force in the line is 1000 kg, the bending stress in the chord is 1.8 times the allowable stress. But we should be aware that allowable bending stress will actually be much lower than this due to the axial stresses in the chords due to the other loads applied to the truss, such as lights, PA or whatever.

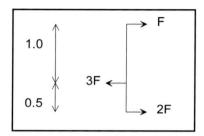

If the line is secured onto a single post which is attached to the top and bottom chord of one side of the truss, then what happens? The posts are (say) 1 metre high with a force, F at the top, then the forces in the connections to the top and bottom chords in a 0.5 metre deep truss are 3F and 2F respectively.

We established earlier that the force in the line could be between 1000 and 2000 kg (9.81 and 19.62 kN), so therefore the force added into the chord top chord could be as much as 6 tonnes, if indeed the connection is strong enough to transfer these forces without breaking.

But can the truss sustain these additional loads? The allowable static equivalent force in the chord of a typical 0.5 metre (20 in) truss with 50.8 mm (2 in) diameter chords and bolted connections is approximately 2500 kg (24.5 kN). But with the large factors of safety that most truss manufacturers have up their sleeves, all is well - or is it? What if the truss is spanning 12 metres (40 ft) and carries 1250 kg (12.26 kN) of lights? Well, the force in the chord at the centre of the span is probably in excess of 2000 kg (19.62 kN) due to the self weight of the truss and the weight of the lights. So suddenly just when your life depends on it, the force in the chord is up to 8000 kg (78.5 kN). Still feeling confident?

One could very quickly imagine a scenario where the loads from the fall arrest equipment could overload the truss and cause the truss itself to fail. Even if the fall doesn't kill you, the collapsing truss structure could.

A fairly convincing argument now starts to develop which suggests that fall arrest equipment should have its own truss grid and that it should not be used on trusses which are used to support lights, PA and the like.

There is an argument in structural engineering circles that the factor of safety against failure in extreme conditions could be reduced as low as 1.05 for steel and concrete buildings. The cost of buildings would be increased considerably if one had to design buildings to sustain a column being blown out by a bomb but still have the usual factors of safety. The building would be badly damaged, but would not collapse. It is accepted that the bomb damage may result in the subsequent demolition of the building. However, fall arrest systems should be seen as last resort life saving equipment and hence there is an argument for keeping normal safety factors. In the above example, failure is a very real possibility and the 8000 kg (78.5 kN) in the chord would probably cause catastrophic results.

It is worth considering exactly how these systems are attached to truss structures. The fixing could be by the use of half couplers common in the scaffold industry or by bolts which sandwich plates on either side of the chord. Both of these methods rely on human vigilance - how tight are the bolts in the half couplers, has the appropriate torque been applied to the bolts?

We also should consider if any other loads could be applied to the truss in the event of an accident. If fall arrest equipment is used on a truss, then one ought to consider how a person is rescued in the event of a fall. One could argue that the truss should be checked for two additional point loads positioned anywhere, which would be equivalent to two 'standard' persons. Clearly, the large loads in the truss which would be induced from the horizontal line due to the arrest of the fall will dissipate quickly and can be considered as a very short term load. The point loads from the rescuers will not coincide with the large forces in the horizontal line due to the arrest of the fall.

Needless to say, if the truss structure has been subjected to loads from fall arrest equipment, then it should be taken out of service and checked by a qualified person before it is used again.

Another possibility of securing the ends of the safety lines would be to an 'O' ring at the hoist position. What do we need to consider here? There is obviously the need to look at the possible pulling of the load through the clutches or brakes on chain hoist and exactly to what the hoist itself is attached. It is not surprising to learn that many chain hoist manufacturers have outlawed the attachment of safety lines to the hoist.

There will be a temptation to simply attach the lines to the existing building. It is clear that the forces can be large and hence full consideration of the resulting reaction is necessary. The lines may be nearly horizontal initially, but they will be at a much different angle when the load is at its greatest. For example, for a span of 18 metres (60 ft), the minimum clearance required below the line is over 8 metres (25 ft). The angle of the line is therefore approaching 45 degrees. All anchorage points should therefore be checked for all possible angles of load by a qualified person.

Wind loads are difficult to assess with the same accuracy as say loads imposed by lighting and sound equipment. The wind loads are dependant on, amongst other things, the shape of the structure, the height above ground, the terrain, and the size, shape and proximity of surrounding buildings. Clearly, these parameters are very difficult to model mathematically and hence a number of assumptions are made which tend to over estimate the wind forces.

For structures in the entertainment industry in the UK, we tend to design for wind loads using one of two distinct approaches. Firstly, we could design on site-specific basis to determine design wind speed and hence pressure and force in accordance with the appropriate codes and standards. However, the structures are generally used at a number of locations and the derivation of forces using a site specific design wind speed is not appropriate. Hence the second approach is also used where the design is based on a given maximum allowable wind speed, without using probability factors, to determine pressure and force. This method is more suited to the entertainment industry where a maximum mean wind speed could be set at say 40 mph, above which the concert would be cancelled.

A few points about wind forces are worth mentioning. Firstly, the force due to wind is proportional to the square of the speed. So it can be seen that the force on a structure due to a 40 mph wind is four times the force due to a 20 mph wind. Secondly, the gust wind speed is approximately 1.6 to 1.9 times the mean wind speed depending on location. Thirdly, and very importantly, all outdoor structures should be designed to resist loads due to wind on items such as banners, hoardings, sound equipment, lighting equipment etc. which may be suspended attached to them.

The subject of wind loads is discussed in greater detail in the section about outdoor structures and roof top structures.

What happens if a motor fails? There can be tendency for people to consider that structures are 'over engineered' when they are designed against the possibility of motor failure. However it should be recognised that this is a very case sensitive topic and one where 'engineering judgement' and thorough risk assessment is critical.

We have discussed the origins and values of 'factors of safety' for aluminium structures. One could argue that the failure of one motor would be an accidental occurrence and hence a reduced factor of safety for the remainder of the structure would be acceptable. This is a common form of design load case for multi-storey buildings to address the issue of progressive collapse. The building would be designed as normal to the appropriate codes and then the stability checked when one of the columns at ground level is removed to simulate a bomb blast. The remainder of the structural frame is checked to ensure that no element actually collapses.

Now take a simple example of a single truss which is supported at three positions - the middle and each end - and carries a uniformly distributed load. Tables exist in engineering text books which define the bending moments and shear forces associated with loads on multi-span beams.

The design of the truss would be checked as normal to ensure that the maximum allowable bending moment and shear force are not exceeded.

Now assume that the central motor failed to function properly and did not provide any support to the truss. The tables show that the bending moment would be a maximum over the central support and would be 0.125WL where W is the total load and L is the span (the distance between supports.) If the central support was removed the span would double and the bending moment would increase by a factor of four.

But what would happen if one of the end motors failed? One side of the truss would be required to cantilever from the position of the central motor. The bending moment at the centre of the truss would then be 0.5WL.

Now consider what would happen if the truss was being lowered and the central motor stopped but the two outer motors continued to function. The chain in the outer motors would go slack and the truss would be required to cantilever from the central support and the bending moment would be 0.5WL.

So we can see that if one of the motors fails the bending moment in the truss would increase dramatically and this would become an accidental load case where a reduced factor of safety could be considered acceptable. Otherwise, the truss would be massively 'over engineered' and over designed to withstand the normal design loads assuming three supports.

In this case a truss being designed to carry a uniform load would have to have an increased factor of safety in normal operating conditions to cater for the accidental load case with one of the motors failing as the bending moment increases by a factor four.

We can see that the normal factors of safety used in truss design of 2:1 or 3:1 are clearly inadequate.

One also has to consider the additional loads at the remaining motors should one motor fail. This may overload either the remaining motors or the existing building, or both. If the remaining motors are overloaded, then the brakes and clutches may slip which could cause the truss the fall.

One has to consider the risks of motor failure when assessing the adequacy of the truss or designing a structural system. If the failure of one motor could cause catastrophic failure or an unacceptably high risk of failure then consideration should be given to installing devices known as 'inertia safeties'. The whole system may start to be impractical if inertia safeties are fixed to each motor position.

I was involved in the design of two 40 metre long walkways for a concert tour which enabled the members of the band to access the B stage from the A stage by way of the walkways which were suspended from the roof of the venue. The walk ways were positioned directly over the audience during the show and they were raised and lowered when access to and from the B stage was required. The design of the walkways was such that if one motor didn't function correctly the structure still performed satisfactorily. In this particular case, the 'factor of safety' was enhanced by incorporating additional hoists. This course of action was adopted as hundreds of people in the audience were

'Wet Wet Wet' catwalks over audience.

standing under the structure when it was both stationary and moving.

What happens if a round sling fails? The scenarios described above where a motor fails would also be true for the failure of round slings. However, there is another issue which is worthy of note. Round slings are generally made of synthetic fibre which will melt in the event of fire. Secondary suspensions such as steel wires should be employed to back up round slings so that the load will not fall if the round sling fails. It should be noted that the safety wires should be reasonably tight. Otherwise, the load will fall a certain distance before the safety wire takes the load in the event of failure of the round sling. The fall and sudden deceleration of the load will impose a greater load on the wire and the support than the actual dead load.

Statically determinate structures are generally simple structures which can be analysed very easily by resolution of forces.

Statically indeterminate structures are more complex and are analysed using finite element analysis or skeletal frame analysis computer programs for very complicated structures or by the hand methods described below for simple structures.

What about multiple pick points? A continuous truss supported at three or more positions is a simple example of a statically indeterminate structure.

The analysis of a single run of truss which has a number of supports with variable spacing and irregular load patterns can be quite complex. There are three simple methods of analysis of statically indeterminate structures which do not require higher mathematics, namely 'The Area-Moment Method', 'Moment Distribution' and 'Slope-Deflection'. Each method is somewhat long winded and quite tedious. These theories and methods of analysis are normally taught during the first term of a first year structures course at college. For those who are particularly interested, I would suggest that you make reference to standard structural engineering text books.

Fortunately, with modern technology, we are now able to model and analyse such structures very easily on a computer and output bending moment, shear force diagrams and deflected shapes, as well as defining the loads at the supports which are required amongst other things, to determine which chain motor capacity would be required.

A number of people advocate the use of a very simplistic method of determining the reactions at chain hoists by considering the length of truss between supports in turn and calculating the reactions. The reactions from each part are summated to give the reaction at the support. An engineer would say that this method is fundamentally flawed and that one cannot simply treat each section of truss as being simply supported between each pick up point, determine the loads at each support from each section of truss and then sum the loads to determine the load in the chain hoist and subsequently, the roof or other supporting structure. He would probably point out that the truss is continuous and therefore the loading on one section will have an effect on the adjacent spans and that if the above method is used, then incorrect reactions will be determined and these could have catastrophic results.

The following model attempts to provide a simple mathematical method of calculating these loads and give some possible explanations of why we have not had a stream of accidents where continuous runs of truss with multiple pick up points have suffered near failure or collapse.

Let us consider a continuous truss of two equal spans with three support points with central point loads on each of the spans.

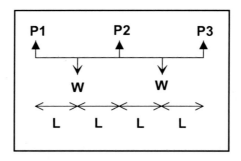

The very simplistic method outlined above would suggest that P1 = P3 = 0.5W and that P2 = 1.0 W

Standard engineering text books state that

This shows that there is an inaccuracy of nearly 40% for the load on the

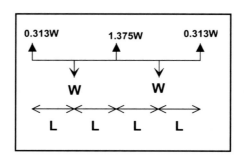

central and outer pick up points between the simplistic method and standard engineering text books.

If we consider a continuous truss of two equal spans with three support points with uniformly distributed loads on each of the spans.

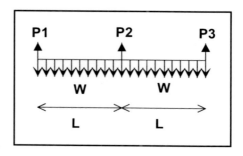

The very simplistic method would suggest that P1 = P3 = 0.5 W and that P2 = 1.0 W

Standard engineering text books state that

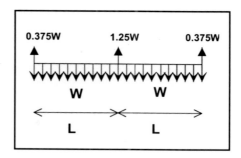

This shows that there is an inaccuracy of some 25% for the load on the central and 33% for the outer pick up point between the simplistic method and standard engineering text books.

There is a quick simple way of determining the bending moment diagram, shear force diagram and the forces at the supports without resorting to high powered mathematics. This is known as Clapeyron's Theorem of Three Moments - a grand title but quite straightforward so there is no need for the latest 2GHz Pentium 4 PC!

The theorem applies only to any two adjacent spans in a continuous beam and is usually applied to a beam or truss of constant stiffness which has all the supports at the same level. This is usually the case for trussing. More complex versions of the theorem can be used for cases where the stiffness of the truss changes along its length.

The proof of the basic theorem results in the following expression:

$$M_A . L_1 + 2 M_B (L_1 + L_2) + M_C . L_2 = 6 (A_1 . X_1 / L_1 + A_2 . X_2 / L_2)$$

where M_A, M_B and M_C are the numerical values of the bending moments at the supports A, B and C respectively and CG denotes the position of the centre of gravity of the free bending moment diagram. The other terms are shown in the following diagram:

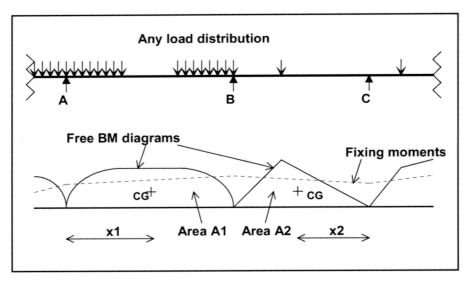

The conditions at the end supports are usually known and these conditions provide the starting points for the solution.

There are three types of end conditions, namely:
1. Simply supported
2. Partially fixed
3. Fully fixed

The shear force at the end of any span is determined after the support moments have been calculated, in the same manner as for a fixed beam, with each span being treated separately. It is essential to note the difference between shear force and the reaction at any support. For example, the shear force at support B due to span AB is a certain amount, while that at support B due to span BC is another amount, but the reaction at the support is the sum of these two amounts.

Let us consider a simple example:

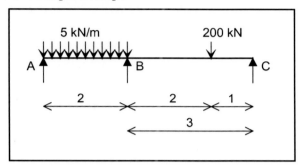

Applying Clapeyron's Theorem and substituting

$L_1 = 2$ m

$L_2 = 3$ m

$$A_1 = \frac{10 \times 2}{8} \times \frac{2 \times 2}{3} = \frac{10}{3} \text{ kNm}^2$$

$$A_2 = \frac{200 \times 1 \times 2}{3} \times \frac{3}{2} = 200 \text{ kNm}^2$$

$x_1 = 1$ m

$x_2 = \dfrac{4}{3}$ m

Therefore

$$M_A . 2 + 2 M_B (2 + 3) + M_C . 3 = 6 \left(\tfrac{10}{3} \times \tfrac{1}{2} + 200 \times \tfrac{4}{3} \times \tfrac{1}{3} \right)$$

A and C are simple supports and therefore

$M_A = M_C = 0$

Therefore

$$M_B = \frac{6}{10} \left(\frac{10}{6} + \frac{800}{9} \right) \quad = 54.33 \text{ kNm}$$

The maximum free bending moment for span AB is
$$w\,L^2/8 = 5 \times 2^2 / 8 = 2.5 \text{ kNm}$$

The maximum free bending moment for span BC is
$$P\,a\,b/L = 200 \times 2 \times 1 / 3 = 133.33 \text{ kNm}$$

The bending moment diagram is therefore

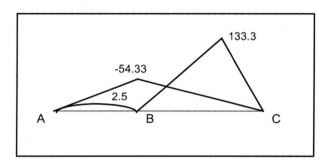

Let the shear force at A, B and C be SF_A, SF_B and SF_C respectively

$$SF_A = 5 + \frac{0 - 54.33}{2} = 5 - 27.17 = -22.17 \text{ kN}$$

$$SF_B \text{ for span AB} = 5 + 27.17 = 32.17 \text{ kN}$$

$$SF_C = \frac{200 \times 2}{3} + \frac{0 - 54.33}{3} = 115.22 \text{ kN}$$

$$SF_B \text{ for span BC} = \frac{200}{3} + 18.11 = 84.78 \text{ kN}$$

Note that the negative reaction at support A means that end A will tend to lift off its support and will have to be held down.

The shear force diagram can now be defined.

The reactions at the supports are therefore
$$R_A = -22.17 \text{ kN}$$

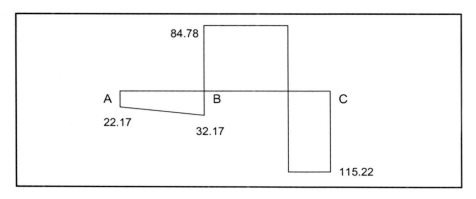

$R_B = 84.78 + 32.17 = 116.95$ kN

$R_C = 115.22$ kN

It is worth noting that if the very simplistic method was used then the reactions would have been determined as

$R_A = 5$ kN

$R_B = 5 + 200 / 3 = 71.67$ kN

$R_C = 2 \times 200 / 3 = 133.33$ kN

It is now apparent that the simplistic method gives potentially dangerous results as the load on the central support is underestimated by nearly 40%.

Now let us consider a more complex example.

This is a three span continuous beam ABCDE which is simply supported at A, cantilevered at D and loaded as shown above.

Applying Clapeyron's theorem

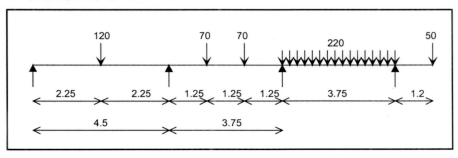

$M_A = 0$ kNm

$M_D = 50 \times 1.2 = 60$ kNm

$A_1 = \dfrac{120 \times 4.5}{4} \times \dfrac{4.5}{2} = 303.75$ kNm²

$A_2 = \dfrac{70 \times 3.75}{3} \times \dfrac{3.75 \times 2}{3} = 218.75$ kNm²

$A_3 = \dfrac{220 \times 3.75}{8} \times \dfrac{3.75 \times 2}{3} = 257.81$ kNm²

First consider spans AB and BC

$M_A + 2 M_B (4.5 + 3.75) + M_C \times 3.75$

$$= 6 \left(\dfrac{(303.75 \times 2.25)}{4.5} + \dfrac{(218.75 \times 1.875)}{3.75} \right)$$

But

$M_A = 0$

Therefore

$16.5 M_B + 3.75 M_C = 1567.5$ Equation 1

Now consider spans BC and CD

$M_B \times 3.75 + 2 \times M_C (3.75 + 3.75) + (M_D \times 3.75)$

$$= 6 \left(\dfrac{(218.75 \times 1.875)}{3.75} + \dfrac{(257.81 \times 1.875)}{3.75} \right)$$

But

$M_D = 60$ kNm

Therefore

$3.75 M_B + 15 M_C + (60 \times 3.75) = 6 (109.375 + 128.905)$

$3.75 M_B + 15 M_C = 1204.68$ Equation 2

Solving the simultaneous equations 1 and 2

$M_B = 81.25$ kNm

$M_C = 59.97$ kNm

So the bending moment diagram is now

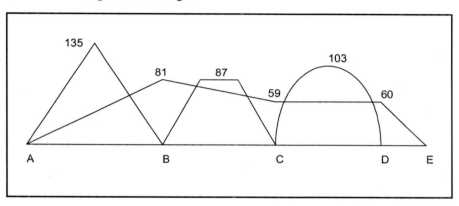

Let the shear force at A, B, C and D be SF_A, SF_B, SF_C and SF_D respectively

$SF_A = \dfrac{120}{2} + \dfrac{0 - 81.25}{4.5} = 60 - 18.05 = 41.95$ kN

SF_B for span AB $= 60 + 18.05 = 78.05$ kN

SF_B for span BC $= 70 + \dfrac{81.25 - 59.97}{3.75} = 70 + 5.675 = 75.675$ kN

SF_C for span BC $= 70 - 5.675 = 64.325$ kN

SF_C for span CD $= \dfrac{220}{2} + \dfrac{59.97 - 60}{3.75} = 110 - 0.008 = 109.992$ kN

SF_D for span CD $= 110 + 0.008 = 110.008$ kN
The shear force diagram can now be defined.

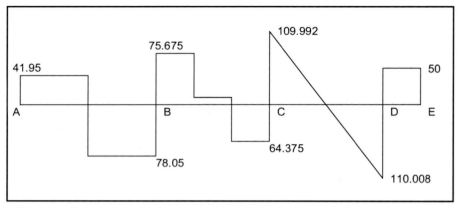

The reactions at the supports are therefore

$$R_A = 41.95 \text{ kN}$$

$$R_B = 78.05 + 75.675 = 153.725 \text{ kN}$$

$$R_C = 64.375 + 109.992 = 174.367 \text{ kN}$$

$$R_D = 110.008 + 50 = 160.008 \text{ kN}$$

So we now have a simple method of determining the reactions at the chain hoists for a continuous run of truss.

But why has there not been a string of near failures or collapses where continuous runs of truss have been used with multiple pick up loads? It is quite difficult for an engineer to answer this question - just where does theory meet reality?

In theory, motors should run at the same speed under a given load - but this is often not the case in practice. If motors are unevenly loaded, they often run at slightly different rates. Both these phenomena can lead to the support points being out of plane which induces bending moments in the truss. These bending moments induce deflections in the truss so that it can take up a shape to suit the level of the pick up points. It is worth considering how much a truss deflects under payload and then realise that similar forces and moments are induced when the support points are out of level. So it is clear that keeping the pick up points level is probably just as important as correctly assessing the load on a truss. Conversely, it is possible to redistribute bending moments by 'bumping' the motors causing the supports to be out of level.

The tolerance in the connections may also be such that full bending moment continuity is not achieved at the support points and some rotation of the plane of the truss is permitted. This again will cause some redistribution of bending moment in the truss and will result in the continuity of the truss at the support points being reduced. This is clearly dependant on the type of connection being used to join two adjacent truss modules. Flexing of the end plates in a truss with a bolted connection may result in some redistribution of bending moment. If the truss module are connected using fork ends and shear pins, then the lack of fit of the pins in the elements may also allow some rotation of the truss and hence redistribution of bending moment. This is an interesting point - if the pins are tight, then users often complain that the truss modules are difficult to connect together, but the truss does not suffer from sagging to the same extent as when the pins are slack.

The use dynamometers is worthy of comment. These are often used to measure the reaction at the support points to ensure that these points are not overloaded. This is a good way of checking that the system is behaving as anticipated.

So what do we conclude from these observations? Professional engineers would say that structural calculations should be carried by a competent person to check that the truss or the support points are not overloaded. Rigging companies would probably point to the fact that they have always done it this way and have never had a problem.

Just where does theory meet reality? The answer is probably somewhere in the middle. Riggers and engineers need to hang together... if they don't, then they may well end up hanging separately!

The above has shown that the distribution of bending moment and shear force for a continuous beam with multiple supports is considerably different from a simply supported beam with two supports. The bending moment is significantly less in mid spans than if the beam was simply supported. But we should not be tempted to propose to use a truss with a lower bending strength. Why? You will find that moments at supports can be quite high and will be opposite in direction to the mid span moments. The change in direction of the bending forces may be critical if a triangular truss is being proposed. You will also find that some of the shear forces at the internal supports may be higher than you may expect. So we can again see that the accurate assessment of

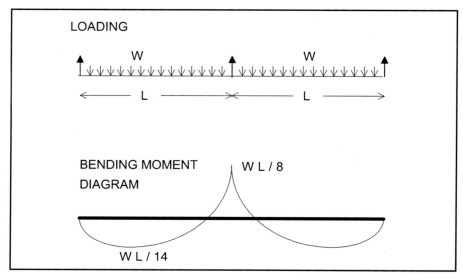

load and the subsequent analysis is critical to the structural stability.

What about the situation when the load moves? Engineers are required to check structures which are subjected to loads which move, for example like a train going across a bridge. A similar example in the entertainment industry would be items of scenery being moved along a track which is suspended at numerous positions from a truss.

As the load moves and passes the various supports, the bending moment and shear forces change along the truss. The values of bending moment and shear force can be assessed at a given position as the load passes along the truss and the maximum and minimum values determined. It is then possible to undertake this analysis at a number of other positions and then plot an envelope of the values of bending moment and shear force. These envelopes of effects are then used to check if the truss is adequate.

Here again, the assessment of the effects of the loads as they move along the truss is critical to the structural stability of the system.

The geographical location also needs to be considered, with particular reference to seismic activity. California is one of the most seismically active areas of the world and has over 10,000 earthquakes each year. Whilst the vast majority of these are small, highly destructive earthquakes do occur, the last of which was centred in Northridge (north west of Los Angeles) in 1994. It caused billions of dollars worth of damage. The American standard ASCE 7 defines loads associated with seismic activity in various areas of the US and also provides information on the combination of design loads such as wind load, seismic load, live load, etc. This document was significantly updated after the Northridge earthquake. It should be appreciated that structures in the most seismically active areas are required to resist both horizontal and vertical loads. Therefore, seismic loading can be a relevant design load case for simple truss runs or grids, as well as more complex structures.

It has been found that seismic loading in combination with other load cases, as set out in ASCE 7, is not normally the most onerous load case for lightweight, temporary structures.

Seismic activity can occur at any time – there is not an "earthquake season". Therefore, the possible reduction in loading associated with seismic activity, due to the short period where a temporary structure is erected, is not normally considered.

Other countries, such as Japan and New Zealand, have their own design standards that cover seismic loading. All these standards are under constant review as engineers' understanding of structural behaviour during seismic events increases.

Total Structures has supplied two large ground supported structures to a Japanese client in 2002 and 2003. These incorporated additional bracing in both the horizontal and vertical planes to resist seismic loads. These can be seen in the photograph below.

The accurate assessment of loads on structures is clearly critical if the inherent factors of safety are not to be eroded. We would suggest 'if in doubt, ask'. But who? A 'competent person' - but who is that? - "a qualified person who, by possession of a recognised degree or certificate of professional standing, or who by extensive knowledge training and experience has successfully demonstrated the ability to solve problems relating to the subject matter and work."

8 EXISTING STRUCTURES

We talked earlier about factors of safety of existing buildings and it is important to consider how individual trusses and truss grids are supported. This is generally the responsibility of the User.

The structural calculations for a grid, or other system which supports lighting and associated equipment, should identify all the loads which are present at the supports and the exact position of the supports which are required. These are generally just straight vertical loads, but can involve both vertical and horizontal loads as well as bending moments.

Clearly, due consideration should be given to any dynamic effects when the grid is supported from the existing structure by chain motors, which is usually the case. The application of a dynamic magnification factor to the static load has been discussed above.

When checking the existing structure, due consideration should be given to both the primary and secondary effects on the elements of the structure.

It is common for existing modern arena buildings or venues to have a set

Load point in existing roof structure

of structural calculations which identify where loads can be applied. These are generally available from the owner of the building or from the Building Control Department of the Local Authority in the UK or the equivalent in other countries.

Sir Issac Newton said "For every action has an equal and opposite reaction" This is true for the structure to be stable. The existing structure should be checked from the place where the additional loads are applied right down to the foundations which support the whole structure.

The loads should be checked at the position where they are applied, usually the roof, the building columns should be checked to ensure that they can sustain the additional loads, and finally the capacity of the foundations should also be considered.

Usually, such a detailed check is not necessary as the owner of the building can identify where loads can be applied and the maximum value of the loads applied at those positions and is, in many cases, legally responsible for ensuring checks are made before loads are imposed.

Occasionally, aluminium structures are rigidly attached to buildings that are located in seismically active areas. For example, the new acoustic canopy is attached to the main steel roof trusses of the Hollywood Bowl, Los Angeles by a number of large steel struts. The project is due for completion in April 2004. The design of the canopy has to account for the behaviour of the main roof structure under seismic and differential thermal loading.

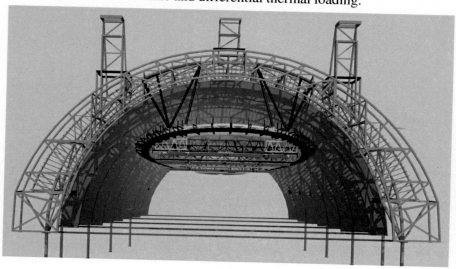

9

TOWER STABILITY THEORY AND GROUND SUPPORT

Sometimes the roof of an existing building cannot support the loads which are required to be carried. In these cases, a structure is required to be placed inside the building to carry these loads. This structure would comprise a grid supported by towers, and this is known as a "ground support".

It is important to understand the theory behind the design of towers when considering ground support and roof top systems. So let us start with Clause 4.7.4.2 and Table 4.8 from BS 8118 'The Structural Use of Aluminium'.

End condition 3	Effectively held in position at both ends, but not restrained in direction.	$K = 1.0$
End condition 4	Effectively held in position at one end, and restrained in direction at both ends.	$K = 1.25$
End condition 5	Effectively held in position and restrained in direction at one end, and partially restrained in direction but not held in position at the other end.	$K = 1.5$
End condition 6	Effectively held in position and restrained in direction at one end, but not held in position or restrained at the other end.	$K = 2.0$

where K is the effective length factor. This is the number by which the actual length of the strut is multiplied, to determine the effective length. This length is then used to check the overall buckling of the column, strut or tower.

If the towers are set in a goal post configuration, then it can be argued that there is no restraint in direction at the top of the tower in one direction. End condition 6 would apply and the effective length would therefore be 2 times the height.

If the towers are set in a square or rectangular format, then it could be argued that there is some restraint in both directions by virtue of the wheels in the sleeve block. End condition 5 would apply and the effective length would therefore be 1.5 times the height.

If the towers are set in a square or rectangular format and stabilisers and braces are provided at the foot of the tower, then it could be argued that there

is some restraint in both directions at the head of the tower by virtue of the wheels in the sleeve block and restraint in direction at the foot of the tower. End condition 4 would apply and the effective length would therefore be 1.25 times the height.

However, care should be taken to ensure that these stabilisers and braces do not cause an obstruction or other hazard and adequate guarding should be provided as required - something which was not in the location shown in this photograph, as the traffic continued to pass the structure on a busy junction!!

If the head of the towers are provided with restraining guy ropes and the bases are not provided with stabilisers and braces, then the tower could be

Unprotected stabilisers and braces on towers in Korea

considered to be a pinned ended strut. End condition 3 would apply and the effective length would therefore be 1.0 times the height.

In the interests of simplicity, four conditions are considered in the standard calculations for 12" and 18" square towers, namely 1) when there are two towers acting as a goal post with adequate base restraint, 2) when there are four towers used in a rectangular or square grid with no stabilisers or braces to provide base restraint 3) when there are four towers used in a rectangular or square grid with stabilisers and braces to provide base restraint and 4) when the heads of the towers are adequately restrained with guy wires.

The effective height of the towers in these configurations is therefore taken in these calculations as 2 times, 1.5 times, 1.25 times and 1.0 times the height of the tower.

When the towers are not guyed, an allowance must be made for sway by assuming towers must be able to sustain a horizontal load at tower top of a percentage of the vertical load in either of two orthogonal directions (that is at right angles to each other). It is considered that this load will not occur in both orthogonal directions simultaneously. This horizontal load will produce a bending moment in the tower, which will create axial loads in tubes and bolts, thereby reducing the payload.

Reference was made to Clause 10 (c) of BS 449 'The Structural Use of Steelwork in Building' for advice on sway stability.

This states that:

> "To ensure adequate strength, in addition to designing for applied horizontal loads, a separate check shall be carried out for notional horizontal forces which can arise due to practical imperfections such as lack of verticality".

> "The notional horizontal forces shall be applied at each roof and floor level or their equivalent and shall be taken as equal to 0.5 per cent of the sum of the dead and imposed gravity loads applied at that level, but not less than 1.0 per cent of the dead load".

> "The notional horizontal forces shall be taken as acting simultaneously with the vertical loads. They shall be assumed to act in any one horizontal direction at one time".

When the towers are not guyed, an allowance must be made for sway by assuming the towers must be able to sustain a horizontal load at tower top of 0.75% of vertical load in either of two orthogonal directions. 0.75% is an arbitrary figure in the range recommended by BS 449 'The Structural Use of Steelwork in Building'. This horizontal load will produce a bending moment in the tower, which will create axial loads in tubes and bolts, thereby reducing the payload.

A sway force can be generated by a lack of verticality. If we assume that the towers could be 100 mm out of plumb at 13.5 metres high, then the angle of the tower would be 0.424 degrees. The tangent of this angle is 0.0074. Therefore the sway force would be 0.75%.

It is reasonable to suggest that towers shall not be used when they are more than 75 mm out of plumb at a height of 13.5 metres. This equates to 50 mm out of plumb at 9 metres.

Although you can generally tell by eye when a tower is out of plumb, you

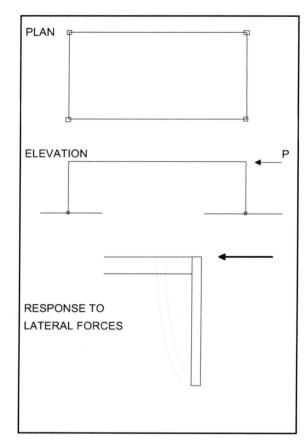

PLAN

ELEVATION   P

RESPONSE TO
LATERAL FORCES

should not rely on this method. The verticality of a tower can easily be checked using a plumb line attached to the sleeve. To facilitate this check, the line should be attached to the sleeve before the grid or roof is raised.

When attaching this line, it is also beneficial to attach a tape measure to each sleeve, so that you can check if the grid is horizontal. The grid should be checked every few metres as it climbs the towers as recommended in the Operating Manuals which will be discussed shortly.

If the grid is raised when it is not horizontal, it will have a tendency to push the towers out of plumb.

Ground support

Ground support is the name given to a grid structure which is supported on a number of towers. The grid is usually constructed at ground level and then self climbs up the towers by way of electric chain motors.

The grids are often rectangular with internal box or ladder trusses.

Internal ground support systems are not generally guyed. They remain stable by virtue of the moment connection which is generated between the sleeve block and the tower. This uses the same principal as a table – which will not topple over sideways unless the legs rip out of the underside of the table top.

Clearly, if the sleeve is not tight on the chords of the tower, then the grid can move to one side before it locks or jams on the towers. This lateral may be very significant and could induce high bending moments and force in the towers.

If the trusses are not very stiff and deflect a large distance under load and the sleeves are tight on the towers then some rotation occurs at the joint. This rotation of the end of the truss induces bending in the tower, and the phenomenon needs to be taken into consideration where high loads are applied to ground support grids. The amount of rotation is a function of the relative stiffness of the towers and the truss, the height of the towers and span of the truss and the amount of applied load.

We talked about sway moment in towers a little earlier. It is the connection of the truss to the tower via the sleeve which transfers this moment.

The diagram opposite shows the general principles of ground support and shows how the forces and moments are generated.

This appears to be fairly explanatory. But quite how the 'ground support system' shown in the following photographs remains stable is unknown.

There is a minimal connection between the tower and the sleeve section and hence there can be virtually no moment transfer between the grid and

Sleeve without wheels on a tower.

Tower with additional chords.

the tower or vice versa. One presumes that some level of fixity at the base of the towers is required for stability to be achieved.

Another manufacturer appreciated that the reaction from the sleeve wheels on the tower could cause local bending in the chords and hence added a third "chord" on two faces to spread the load. This is of questionable benefit as the sway moment and therefore the load on the tower could be in either of the two orthogonal directions and that the additional chords were only provided in the top part of the uppermost tower module. Indeed the sway moment in the tower reduces linearly between top and bottom of the tower, assuming a 'pinned' base. Therefore the sway moment is some 50% of the maximum at mid height of the tower.

When ground support systems are used outdoors, it is usual that they are provided with guy ropes.

But why outdoors and not indoors? Well this is subject to engineering calculations, which is, of course, true of all structures. After all, we are dealing with large pieces of equipment which, if they fell down, could cause damage, injury or death. You should not guess if a structure is adequate - artistes and the public have a right to expect more than that.

The structure itself will attract lateral loading when the wind blows. The addition of such things as lighting and sound equipment, hoarding, banners, weather protection and the like to a structure can attract a substantial amount of wind load which can have a significant effect on the stability of the structure in adverse weather conditions.

The towers will have been checked to ensure that they can resist the vertical loads from the grid. However, the standard calculations which are produced by manufacturers generally do not check for the lateral bending induced from wind loads applied to a ground support or roof structure. This check must be carried out by the user to ensure that the towers are strong enough to resist the bending moment induced in them from the lateral force applied at grid level - it is very common to find that they will not unless guy ropes are used to resist the horizontal forces at grid level, so eliminating bending in the tower due to wind loads.

If the structure is guyed then it cannot move laterally at the grid level and hence sway induced bending moments and wind induced bending does not occur in the towers, providing of course the guys are adequate.

If one or more of the towers settles or subsides due to poor ground conditions, then this could cause rotation of the tower and induce high sway forces due to lack of verticality. The subject of ground conditions and how they affect structures is discussed at length in the next chapter.

10 GROUND CONDITIONS, FOUNDATIONS AND ANCHORS

"Whoever, then, hears these commandments of mine and carries them out, is like a wise man who built his house upon rock; and the rain fell and the floods came and the winds blew and beat upon that house, but it did not fall; it was founded upon rock. But whoever hears these commandments and does not carry them out is like a fool, who built his house upon sand; and the rain fell and the floods came and the winds blew and beat upon that house, and it fell; and great was the fall of it."

Matthew 7:24-27

It has been recognised since long before Biblical times that strong buildings depend on firm foundations — if the foundations prove inadequate, the structures fall — and this is just as true for ground support grids, roofs and similar structures used in concerts and other touring events. These structures are used in a wide variety of situations, both indoors and outdoors. Floors should be relatively predictable, but if a structural system is to be used outside, then it is important to consider the ground underneath the structure. The minds of the good and great may have been turned to the superstructures, but if the foundations prove inadequate, then their efforts will all have been in vain. How should we go about this?

There are four main points to consider when evaluating the ground as a support for a structure:

1. How long the structure will be in use?
2. How much the ground will support?
3. How much settlement is tolerable?
4. What conditions might change the ability of the ground to support the load?

The structures used for outdoor concerts and the like are termed demountable structures, and are assembled from modular components for relatively short periods of use, 28 days or less. It is well known that the performance of some types of soil under short-term loading can be significantly different from that when the loads are applied for a longer period. That is to say, settlement usually comprises both immediate and longer term movements. This is generally because the pore water pressures within the soil take time to dissipate. Long term movements need not to be taken into account unless the structures will be in use for more than 28 days, in which case a full engineering assessment of the ground should be made.

Foundation design standards have been written for permanent buildings, which generally have a design life in excess of 50 years. With these permanent structures, settlements, both long term and short term, need to be kept to a minimum. Settlement is often less critical for temporary demountable structures. For example, if a permanent building settles 50 mm in the first month after completion, then damage ranging from broken glazing to structural failure may result, particularly if that rate of settlement continues over the next 599 months of its designed life! If a temporarily erected tower in the corner of concert ground support system settled by 50 mm, there would less cause for concern. The structure is more flexible and tolerant to differential settlement and is dismantled in less than 28 days. Therefore, not all the provisions of these permanent building standards apply to temporary demountable structures.

How much the ground will support is first addressed by considering the allowable bearing pressures, which are linked to the amount of settlement anticipated. The allowable bearing pressure on the ground is determined by

Bearing Surface	Allowable Bearing Pressure kN/m² (lb/ft²)
Dense Sand	200 (4,177)
Medium Dense Sand	150 (3,133)
Loose Sand	100 (2,088)
Stiff Clay	150 (3,133)
Firm Clay	100 (2,088)

Table 1: Indicative values of allowable bearing pressures for different surfaces for structures in place for less than 28 days.

taking the pressure that is likely to cause failure of the ground and multiplying it by an appropriate design factor of less than 1. This yields an allowable bearing pressure at which unacceptable movement of the foundation is highly unlikely to occur. Loadings from structures must be distributed and the foundations must be sized so that any bearing pressures are within this limit.

Allowable bearing pressures should not exceed the values given in Table 1, unless this has been justified by site testing. If test data are not available or if there is doubt about the uniformity of the site conditions, the pressures in Table 1 may require to be adjusted by a competent person. In the absence of reliable local or professional engineering knowledge, a bearing pressure not exceeding 50 kN/m² (1044 lb./ft.²) should be assumed.

It should be appreciated that these traditional values of allowable bearing pressures may not be appropriate where the supports to temporary structures use small baseplates or sole plates. These types of foundation impose virtual point loads on the ground. The point loads exerted by the structure should not exceed the allowable point loads. Guidance is provided in Table 2 on the allowable loads on small 150 mm square and 250 mm square soleplates on typical soils.

The ground surface on which temporary structures are positioned may

	Allowable Load	
Bearing Surface	**150mm sq. (6" square) kN (lb)**	**250mm sq. (9 ³/₄" square) kN (lb)**
Dense Sand	10.5 (2,400)	30 (6,700)
Medium Dense Sand	7 (1,600)	20 (4,500)
Loose Sand	3.5 (800)	10 (2,200)
Stiff Clay	7 (1,600)	20 (4,500)
Firm Clay	3.5 (800)	10 (2,200)

Table 2: Indicative values of allowable vertical loads on adequate sole plates for different surfaces for structures in place for less than 28 days.

include gravel paths, pastures, heaths, sports fields, concrete or asphalt surfaced areas, and the like. Before they are accepted for carrying the design loads, the suitability of such surfaces should be visually checked by a competent person, augmented as necessary by a desk study, trial pits, or by ground investigation involving soil tests or load tests, and taking account of local knowledge.

Particular care should be taken where structures are supported on asphalt or concrete paving. The thickness and type of surface and underlying material are critical to the ability of the surface to support loads. One may be tempted to think that a car park would make an ideal location for a stage and must be able to carry the weight, since cars seem so heavy. However, one should realise that such areas are frequently designed to carry a load of 2.5 kN/m^2 (52 lb./ft.^{2}) — one third the rating of many professional theatre stages. They may also be designed for point loads of no more than 9kN (2,000 lb.) and the surfaces may be comparatively thin, so they would be unable to support the large point loads of many temporary structures.

Some other surfaces may also pose problems. No supports should be founded on backfilled ground that has been excavated locally, unless the granular fill has been properly compacted. Peat and organic subsoils are unsuitable for foundations under any circumstance. Underground services may also be a problem. The event organiser should notify the user of the position of underground services that may present hazards during the build up or use of the structure. If underground services cross the site where the structure is to be erected, the client should obtain advice from the service company concerned. It would be prudent to make a telephone available on site to call emergency services if required.

The normal method of support for stages, grandstands and similar demountable frames where the loads are relatively small is to place timber soleplates on the ground and then use scaffolding screw jacks with steel base plates to take up differences in level. Soleplates and grillages (frameworks of crossed beams for spreading the load over a larger area) should be engineered and not left to chance. Experience has shown that the use of timber or plywood soleplates is generally satisfactory. Concentrated baseplate loads can be assumed to spread through the timber soleplate at 2 horizontal to 1 vertical along the grain, and 1 to 1 across the grain, unless proven otherwise by calculation. With plywood one must consider the plywood in bending. The manufacturers of plywood will provide the values of allowable bending stresses in their documentation. An important point to note is that the allowable stresses are greatly reduced with high moisture contents, which are likely with plywood that is in contact with the ground.

If the site slopes or is uneven, the ground should be made flat or the structure should be capable of being modified to deal with the unevenness. Where the ground is not level or near level and the foundation bases for the structure cannot be set at an angle, measures should be taken to provide a level base. This may be done by cutting steps into the ground or laying timber sleepers up the slope with timber blocks shaped to match the slope, nailed to these to form individual foundations for each upright. Cutting steps in the soil is also a way of removing springy turf, which may provide an unstable footing otherwise. In any case, care is required to obtain full and even contact with the ground. Depressions should be filled and loose material compacted.

The greatest risk of foundation failure is because of unequal settlement. Soft spots due to peat, unconsolidated fill, cavities, drains, and previous excavations can cause unequal settlement that sets up high stresses and deformations in the structure. The position of the supports should therefore be set out on site and any soft spots which coincide with the support positions should be filled and compacted or bridged with grillages or other suitable transfer structures.

Some large structures, such as roofs, video screen support frames, and circus tents are supported on towers. Tower structures are particularly sensitive to differential settlements that may cause tilting of the structure. If the towers are not vertical, then bending stresses are induced which could lead to excessive forces in the chords and diagonals of the towers, eventually leading to failure.

Large galvanised steel plates are sometimes used to spread the load at the base of a tower.

Handles are provided in the example shown in the following photograph to enable the plate to be carried more easily.

When making any assessment of the ground, consideration should be given to anything that could change its condition. The principal factor would probably be the prevailing weather conditions. For example, frozen or dried out ground will support higher pressures than the same ground when it has thawed or wet. Flooding can reduce the load bearing capacity of the ground or wash away the ground under the supports. Particular care should be taken when positioning rain water pipes from roof structures. They should discharge

Base of tower with plate

well away from and below the main structural supports. Where there is a possibility that water could soften the ground or cause scouring, then a suitably hard foundation should be prepared that is deep and wide enough to prevent it being undermined during the time the structure is in use.

One other thing to consider is that not all forces are vertical and downward. The possibility that a foundation might also have to resist horizontal forces or a net uplift should also be considered. Adequate resistance to sliding and uplift should be provided, with a minimum design factor of 1.5. That is, the foundation should be able to resist a force at least 1.5 times greater than any anticipated sliding or uplift force.

Where there are sliding or uplift forces, it is necessary to provide an attachment to the ground using ground anchors at the support points. The manufacturers of commercially available ground anchors usually provide data on allowable working loads for various soil types, and also provide guidance and recommendations for installation. It should be noted that these allowable loads vary considerably. The Health and Safety Executive in the UK has undertaken research into ground anchors and reference should be made to their report entitled 'Factors affecting the load carrying capacity of ground anchors used to support temporary structures' published in February 1998.

Given the variability of the effectiveness of ground anchors in different soils, consideration should be given to on-site testing. This may instill confidence in their holding capacity, and the testing can be done by means of a forklift with a calibrated load cell. It is important that the angle of the test load matches the direction in which the real load will be applied. A suitable design factor should be applied to the ultimate failure load using this method in order to establish the allowable tensile load.

Occasionally, it is not possible to provide ground anchors due the nature of the ground, for example, asphalt, block paving, or concrete. In such cases, the structure should be restrained by ballast of sufficient weight to resist the vertical and horizontal components of the forces in the guy ropes by a factor of 1.5. The angle of the guy rope and the coefficient of friction between the ballast and the ground surface are critical. If the force in a guy rope at 45 degrees is 3 tons, then the weight of the ballast required could well be in excess of 6 tons, depending on the interface between the ballast and the ground.

In some instances, especially if the temporary structure is to be supplied on a regular basis, it may be advisable to install permanent foundations. These will normally be concrete pads or raft slabs but in practice any form of foundation could be considered, including short-bored piles. In conclusion, while the Leaning Tower of Pisa may have gained international recognition as a result of its unsound foundations, I feel this is the sort of notoriety you should avoid.

11 ADEQUACY OF A TYPICAL GRID STRUCTURE

So how do we check if a ground support grid is adequate?

This is probably best described by running through a worked example.

The structure is to be used indoors only. The type of perimeter and internal trusses are assumed and are then checked to see if they are adequate. The maximum allowable loads for various load configurations are obtained from the load charts.

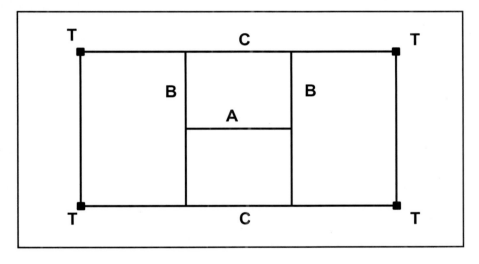

Assume that the overall grid dimensions are 24 by 12 metres and that it is constructed from fold flat truss which has a self-weight of say 20 kg per metre run.

The length of truss A is 8 metres and has an imposed load of 30 kg per metre which makes 240 kg in total.

The towers are positioned at points marked T, are 8 metres high, are unguyed and are constructed from 18" tower sections.

The grid is to be used on many occasions and therefore the factor of 0.85 in the structural calculations for the truss is appropriate. The allowable loads in the published load charts are therefore valid.

The imposed load is to be applied after the whole grid is at trim height by using chain motors and therefore a dynamic magnification factor of 1.25 is deemed to be appropriate. This is only applied to the imposed load as it is only the imposed load which moves. If the load was attached to the grid and then the whole grid lifted, then the dynamic magnification factor would apply to the self weight of the trusses within the grid as well.

The imposed load theoretically becomes 1.25 times 240 = 300 kg. Start with the middle of the grid and check if the truss can sustain the load by comparing the design load with the allowable load in the load charts. From the load charts for fold flat truss, the allowable uniformly distributed load for a span of 9 metres is 3688 kg. Clearly truss A is adequate.

Determine the shear force at each end of the truss. This will include the load due to the self weight of the truss and also the payload. The end reactions from truss A will be half of the self weight of the truss plus half of the imposed load or payload. The end reactions are therefore (8 x 20 / 2) + (300 / 2) = 230 kg. Check if truss B, which supports the truss A, can sustain the reaction from the first truss by comparing the design load with the allowable load in the load charts – in this case, it is a central point load. From the load charts for fold flat truss, the allowable centre point load for a span of 12 metres is 1338 kg. Clearly truss B is adequate

Next determine the shear forces at each end of these trusses which includes the shear force due the self weight of the truss. Check if the perimeter truss can sustain these loads - in this case it will be a third point load. The end reactions from truss B will be half of the self weight of the truss plus half of the payload as it is equally spread over the length of the truss B and not biased towards one end. The end reactions are therefore (12 x 20 / 2) + (230 / 2) =120 + 135 = 255 kg. From the load charts the allowable third point load for a span of 24 metres is 384 kg. Clearly truss C is adequate

Finally, determine the end reactions of the trusses at the sleeve block. Check the towers to see if they can sustain these loads. The load charts for towers are quite complex. There are a number of different charts depending on the arrangement at the base of the tower and if any guys are being used. The end reactions from truss C will be half of the self weight of the truss plus half of the payload as it is equally spread over the length of the truss C and not biased towards one end. The end reactions will therefore be (24 x 20 / 2) + (2 x 255 / 2) = 240 + 255 = 495 kg. The self-weight of the side trusses is

240kg. Therefore the load imposed on the tower is 495 + 240 / 2 = 615kg.

From the load charts for 18" towers in a four tower ground support, 8 metres high with braces and stabilisers at the foot of each tower and unguyed, K = 1.25, is 4538 kg. Clearly the towers are adequate.

This is a simple example. For more complex arrangements of loads and trusses it will be necessary to determine the bending moments and shear forces in the trusses and check these against the maximum allowable bending moments and shear forces for the trusses obtained from the structural calculations.

It is often necessary to undertake a grillage analysis using a linear elastic skeletal frame analysis computer program. For certain types of grids there will be a certain amount of distribution of the loads in both the x and y directions. This is because the shorter spans of truss will tend to 'prop up' the longer spans.

For such types of grids, it is usually necessary for the user to obtain advice, though some rough calculations can be undertaken to determine if the grid is worth analysing further. This advice can generally be obtained from a reputable manufacturer.

We talked earlier about tower stability theory. It would be worth going back to that subject and consider when the payload is applied to a ground support structure.

If the grid is raised off the ground (say) a couple of metres, the towers extend vertically above the sleeve. The chain passes over the top of the head block and hence the load is applied at the top of the tower. Each tower is therefore a vertical cantilever and has an effective length of double its actual height. The allowable load on such a tower is considerably less than when the tower is fully or partially restrained at each end.

You should therefore check if the tower with K = 2 can carry the self weight of the grid plus the payload, with, of course, the 25% additional load due to snatch of the chain motor. If these conditions are not met, then it will be necessary to raise the grid into place before applying the payload.

If the motor is attached to the sleeve, and the chain passes over the pulley block at the tower and down to the sleeve on the other side, then the amount of lift produced is twice the tension in the chain. This is because the tension in the chain is essentially the same on either side of the pulley block, the difference being friction forces between the chain and the pulley and between the pulley, axle and cheek plates. If one uses a 1000 kg hoist in this configuration then a lift of approximately 2000 kg results – a mechanical advantage of 2. The axial force is applied at the top of the tower and is concentric.

You should also check if the motor itself will give sufficient lift, i.e. half the total load on the tower. If not, then you will need to consider lifting the grid to trim height and locking off the grid to the towers before adding the payload.

Some manufacturers offer head blocks or pulley blocks where the distance from the centre of the tower to each pulley position is different. This results in the net load being applied off centre of the tower which in turn means that bending is induced in the tower. As the force from the chains is high, significant bending moments are induced even with low values of offsets. The allowable axial force in the towers should reflect this offset.

If the motor is attached to the base of the tower, and the chain passes over the pulley block and the down to the sleeve, then the axial force in the tower is double the force in the chain. The force in the chain is essentially the weight being lifted. A 1000 kg hoist then lifts 1000 kg but induces 2000 kg in the tower. This is not generally beneficial.

Locking off the grid can take various forms and is generally site-specific.

One possible method of locking off is to rest the grid on a number of tubes of adequate shear and bending strength which pass through the connections in the tower sections which takes the load off the chain and the motor. This method only works where the towers are at the same level. It should be also noted that tubes should not be placed anywhere else other than the connection of tower elements or other parts which are specifically designed to transfer the loads from the grid to the tower. The connections in the tower usually comprise of members of adequate strength, but this should be checked with the manufacturer or the designer.

Another method is to provide additional members (of adequate strength) in the the tower and sleeve that are closed positioned in plan and drilled with a series of holes. When the bolts coincide, bolts are inserted to lock the sleeve to the tower. Having a series of holes allows for some degree of out of level of the towers.

One method that is used where towers are out of level is to pass steel cables over the head block and back down to the sleeve. The grid is lowered so that the load is taken on these wires and is taken off the chain and the motor.

12 OUTDOOR STRUCTURES AND WIND LOADING

When a ground support grid is to be used outdoors, some weather protection is generally required either to keep the rain off the performers and the equipment or to keep the sun off, though this latter scenario is generally not the governing factor in the UK!

A number of manufacturers and rental companies have developed roof systems to address these problems. They take various forms and range from 'sun shades' to substantial structures capable of supporting 20 or 30 tonnes of payload. The designs vary from a ground support structure with inclined trusses to form the gables with an apex truss to form the ridge to fully modular purpose built systems which allow great flexibility in the positioning of pick up points.

Some designs are more successful than others and these two photographs

A roof collapse in Singapore

Alternative view of roof collapse in Singapore

demonstrate that careful consideration of a number of issues is required for a successful outcome.

It would appear that the roof was erected and left overnight. A considerable amount of rain fell and the roof 'ponded' due to inadequate drainage. The volume of the rain water which collected on the skin became so high that the structure was unable to withstand the loading and collapsed.

The roofs manufactured by my own company are often of modular construction and are generally simple to construct. That is to say that they comprise a number of compartments usually 3 metres square and there are a small number of basic components.

The apex of the roof generally runs upstage - downstage and is centrally positioned. The rain will therefore tend to run off to the sides of the roof and not forward towards the audience. The trusses which span across the stage generally slope at about ten degrees to assist in run off of rain water and reduce the possibility of ponding between the trusses.

The perimeter of the roof comprises a conventional truss along the side faces and a combination of sloping box truss and sections of the same truss which is located at the sides on the upstage and downstage faces. PA wings can be added and these are not generally the same depth as the main roof structure.

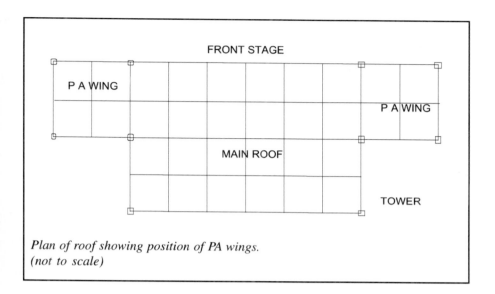

FRONT STAGE

P A WING

P A WING

MAIN ROOF

TOWER

Plan of roof showing position of PA wings.
(not to scale)

Typical roof structure

Roof structure, South Africa

Typical roof structures

There are some very useful diagrams included in the Appendix of the Operating Manual for Roof Structures which show the basic components, the way they fit together and the way the roof is constructed and these are reproduced below.

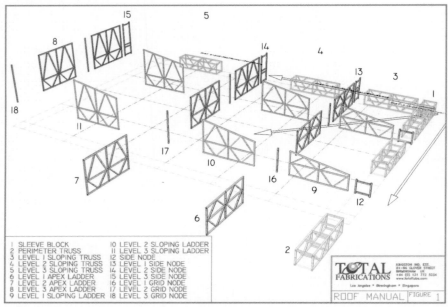

1	SLEEVE BLOCK	10	LEVEL 2 SLOPING LADDER
2	PERIMETER TRUSS	11	LEVEL 3 SLOPING LADDER
3	LEVEL 1 SLOPING TRUSS	12	SIDE NODE
4	LEVEL 2 SLOPING TRUSS	13	LEVEL 1 SIDE NODE
5	LEVEL 3 SLOPING TRUSS	14	LEVEL 2 SIDE NODE
6	LEVEL 1 APEX LADDER	15	LEVEL 3 SIDE NODE
7	LEVEL 2 APEX LADDER	16	LEVEL 1 GRID NODE
8	LEVEL 3 APEX LADDER	17	LEVEL 2 GRID NODE
9	LEVEL 1 SLOPING LADDER	18	LEVEL 3 GRID NODE

TOTAL FABRICATIONS   KINGSTON IND. EST. 81-86 GLOVER STREET BIRMINGHAM UK +44 (0) 121 772 5234 www.totalfabs.com
Los Angeles • Birmingham • Singapore

ROOF MANUAL   FIGURE 1

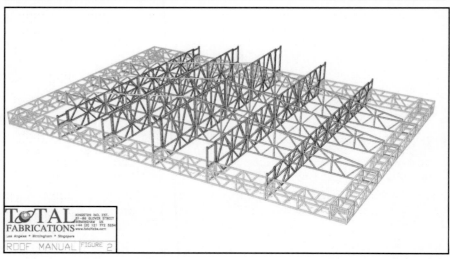

TOTAL FABRICATIONS   KINGSTON IND. EST. 81-86 GLOVER STREET BIRMINGHAM UK +44 (0) 121 772 5234 www.totalfabs.com
Los Angeles • Birmingham • Singapore

ROOF MANUAL   FIGURE 2

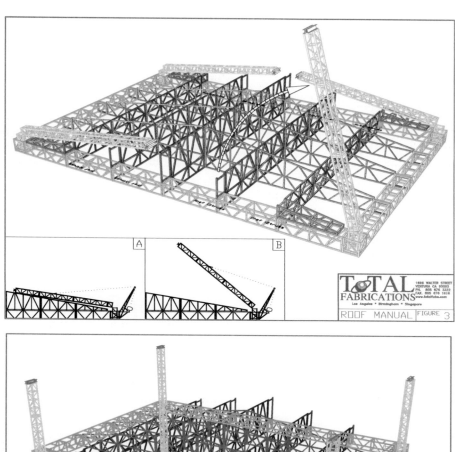

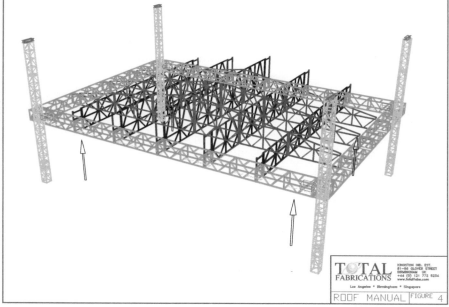

Aluminium Structures in the Entertainment Industry 143

As with complex ground support systems, the roof grid is analysed as a grillage using a linear elastic skeletal frame analysis computer program.

You may recall the incident some time ago where a roof structure collapsed during a show injuring the performer, Curtis Mayfield. The accident has left him crippled. I understand that the structure was not erected in accordance with the original design, the winds were higher than permissible by the manufacturer of the structure and the roof structure was supported by proprietary telescopic towers. These types of tower were originally designed as devices for placing air conditioning ducts inside buildings. They are essentially load placement devices and therefore should not be used as load support devices. The User should always use equipment in accordance with the manufacturer's guidelines and recommendations. If he or she is in any doubt then he should seek advice from a competent person or the manufacturer.

An incident took place in the UK in the summer of 1997 when a delay tower blew down, seriously injuring a young girl. She was given artificial resuscitation at the scene before being taken to hospital where she spent many weeks in intensive care being treated for severe head injuries. The towers were proprietary telescopic units, without, it is understood, the correct deployment of the stabilisers and placed on small raised platforms.

Here are just two very clear reminders that wind loads are critical when considering using temporary structures outdoors and that we must take great care when assessing the loads, checking the adequacy of the structure and monitoring the weather conditions on site.

The loads imposed on structures by, say, lighting and sound equipment are generally easily determined whereas wind loads are difficult to assess with the same accuracy.

Wind loads are dependant on a variety of factors including the geographical location, shape of the structure, the height above ground, the terrain and the size, shape and proximity of surrounding buildings. These parameters affect the flow of air and hence the forces imposed on the various parts of the structure. The parameters are very difficult to model mathematically and hence a number of assumptions are made in the national design standards which tend to be based on empirical rules and model and full scale testing.

For permanent buildings, it is usual to examine the location in which a structure will exist. It is then possible to determine the design wind speed for that location and hence the pressure and force in accordance with the appropriate codes and standards for wind loads.

Before we consider the wind loading on outdoor structures in more detail, let us highlight a number of points regarding wind loads.

Firstly, the force due to wind is proportional to the square of the speed. So it can be seen that the force on a structure due to a 40 mph wind is four times the force due to a 20 mph wind.

Secondly, the three second gust is approximately 1.6 to 1.9 times the mean wind speed depending on location and effective height. It is therefore essential that there is consistency in the definition of wind speed in the structural design calculations and the personnel on site.

Thirdly, and very importantly, all outdoor structures should be designed to resist loads due to wind on items such as banners, hoardings, sound equipment, lighting equipment etc. which may be suspended or attached to them. Wind loads on 'flown' production hardware should be taken into account when checking the overall stability of the structure and when checking the structure is adequate for a given payload configuration. More specifically, consideration should be given to checking the stability of the structure for various combinations of wind and payload to determine the worst case scenario unless specific operating limits are defined in the calculations.

The relationship between metres per second (m/s) and miles per hour (mph) is 10 m/s = 22.37 mph. Clearly, 10 m/s is equivalent to 36 km per hour (kph).

m/s	10	11	12	13	14	15	16	17	18	19	20	21	22	23	24	25
mph	23	25	27	29	31	34	36	38	40	42	45	47	49	51	53	56
kph	36	40	43	47	50	54	58	61	65	68	72	76	79	83	86	90

The table shown overleaf is useful in determining the order of magnitude of the wind. It should however not be used in lieu of an anemometer or other wind speed measuring device.

Hurricanes, cyclones or typhoons are characteristic of tropical regions and these result in winds of higher intensity and probability than those in areas where the weather is governed by general frontal depressions.

It is critical to ensure that structures are only used which are specifically designed for outdoor use. Proprietary equipment should not be used which was designed for load placement indoors for supporting loads outdoors. This point is particularly relevant for structures such as delay towers.

Wind loading is often the most critical load case for an outdoor roof structure particularly if the payload is small. The basic premise chosen is that the structure will not 'fly', blow away or overturn, and this requires that the gravity loads will exceed the uplift forces by an acceptable margin. The critical wind speed is therefore different for each load condition and for the 'attitude' of the roof plane to the wind.

Beaufort Scale	Description	Mean Wind Speed Range m/s at 10m	Effects
B0	Calm	0 - 0.2	
B1	Light Air	0.3 - 1.5	No noticable wind
B2	Light Breeze	1.6 - 3.3	Wind felt on face.
B3	Gentle Breeze	3.4 - 5.4	Wind extends light flag.
B4	Moderate Breeze	5.5 - 7.9	Raises dust and loose paper, hair disarranged, clothing flaps.
B5	Fresh Breeze	8.0 - 10.7	Limit of agreeable wind on land.
B6	Strong Breeze	10.8 - 13.8	Umbrellas used with difficulty, force of the wind felt on the body, wind noisy, frequent blinking.
B7	Near Gale	13.9 - 17.1	Inconvenience felt when walking, difficult to walk steadily, hair blown straight.
B8	Gale	17.2 - 20.7	Generally impedes progress, walking difficult to control, great difficulty with balance in gusts.
B9	Strong Gale	20.8 - 24.4	People blown over by gusts, impossible to face wind, ear ache, headache, breathing difficulty. Some structural damage occurs: falling roof tiles, tree branches, etc. Hazardous for pedestrians.
B10	Storm	24.5 - 28.4	Seldom experienced inland. Trees uprooted, considerable structural damage occurs.

Beaufort Scale

The passage of wind over a duo pitch canopy structure causes uplift on both halves of the roof. The wind on the gables at the front and back of the roof causes lateral forces at roof grid level. A combination of these effects could cause the roof to overturn above a certain wind speed. So guy ropes are provided to prevent this from happening. If they are not provided, then adequate ballast is required at each tower position and the towers need to be designed to resist the bending induced by the application of lateral wind loads.

The structural calculations for roof structures are usually prepared assuming that the area beneath the canopy is only filled part height. The equipment below the canopy should only be filled to half the trim height unless expressly notified by the Client/User before manufacture, as the amount of blockage below the roof affects the wind flow and hence the force on the canopy itself.

It is necessary to consider a number of load cases in the analysis of an outdoor structure. Various combinations of these load cases determine the maximum downward load and the maximum upward load on the roof structure.

If the dead weight of the roof, the rain load and the payload are considered acting together, then this will cause the maximum downward load. The combination of dead load of the roof plus wind load with no payload will result in the maximum upward load.

For roofs with a low design wind speed and hence low uplift forces, it is sometimes possible to impose minimum payloads on the roof structure so that there is no resultant upward load.

The use of walls around a roof structure needs to be carefully considered. The user must notify the designer if he intends to use walls.

Solid back or side walls should comply with the full wind load criteria. The lateral load on a solid back wall of a medium sized roof could amount to a number of tonnes even in relatively low wind speeds. Consideration of the passage of these loads to ground level must be made in the design.

Wind forces on walls which comprise weather wall, scrim or other perforated material should not be discounted. The wind forces on walls comprising such material may be determined for a lower speed than the full design wind speed, if they are removed at that lower wind speed. If this criterion applies the actions required at the critical wind speeds should be clearly stated in the design documentation and in the method statement.

Wind forces on walls which include blow out panels should also be carefully considered. The forces must be determined before and after the panels have blown out, and should be considered as separate load cases when assessing the overall stability of the structure.

Blow out panels can be attached by fixings which fail at a predetermined wind pressure. This pressure is often difficult to establish accurately. Due recognition shall be taken of this in the design calculations. If blow out panels are used, then adequate measures shall be taken to prevent injury or damage when the panels become dislodged.

Two methods of assessing wind loading on temporary structures have emerged in recent years The first was developed in the UK by the IStructE when preparing "Temporary Demountable Structures". The second was adopted by the Task group writing a new ANSI standard BSR E1.21 Temporary Stage roofs. This standard is in the process of preparation and is expected to be published in mid 2004. The Task Group was set up by the Rigging Working Group as part of the Technical Standards Program of ESTA, USA, and comprises representatives from manufacturers and users of temporary stage roofs as well as Professional Engineers.

Let us first consider the approach adopted in the UK, where the weather systems are generally quite predictable.

Wind loading on temporary structures in the UK.

There is no clear provision in BS 6399 Design Loadings for Buildings for the assessment of wind loads on temporary structures.

Structures used in the entertainment industry are generally required to be located in many differing urban/rural environments and there are valid arguments which allow the design for wind loads to be undertaken using one of two distinct approaches.

The first approach is to design on a site specific basis using the same philosophy as for permanent buildings. The derivation of forces using a site specific design wind speed would be admissible for any time of year. Care should be taken when computing the wind pressures as some codes use mean wind speeds whereas others use three second gust speeds. The British Standard for wind loading has been changed in this regard quite recently.

In the UK, January is the windiest month whereas June to August is the calmest period. Generally speaking, the structures would probably be over engineered if they were designed for the full design wind loads using the same philosophy as for permanent buildings for use all year round and then only used during the summer months.

It should be noted that separate calculations would have to be prepared for each site if this approach is used and has financial implications which could affect the viability of small productions.

The second approach which could be used is where the design is based on a given maximum allowable wind speed, without using probability factors, to determine pressure and force. It could be argued that this method is more suited to the entertainment industry where a maximum mean wind speed could be set. When the wind speed approaches this figure a series of procedures are set in motion to prevent damage or injury. Clearly, there is little point in designing structures to withstand say 100 mph winds as the event would have been stopped. and the structures partially or totally dismantled long before the wind reached this speed. This is, of course, assuming that the structure could be partially or totally dismantled or at least the items which attract high wind loads such as covers and walls could be removed. You should consider that the concert will usually be cancelled when the mean wind speed reaches about 40 mph as, for example, it is difficult to hear the PA and walk in open areas above this wind speed.

For this approach to be safe, it is critical that an Operations Management Plan to be prepared and rigorously enforced. This is discussed later in this chapter and an example provided.

Wind loading on temporary structures in the USA.

The weather systems in the USA are less predictable than those in the UK. It is not uncommon for high winds and storms to develop very quickly and without warning.

Section 6 of ANSI 37 Design Loads of Structures during Construction indicates that the design wind speed for structures in place for less than 60 days should be taken as 75% of the full design wind speed for a permanent building. We have seen from above that wind load is proportional to the square of the wind speed. therefore, the design wind loading on temporary structures is assumed to be about half that for permanent buildings.

However, there is an exception to the rule and that deals with areas that are prone to hurricanes. The design wind speed for these areas is in the order of 150 mph. Hurricanes are predictable in the USA and are tracked in great detail from the Gulf to the mainland. There is, therefore, time to dismantle a temporary structure. Hence, the standard suggests that it is reasonable to adopt a basic design wind speed of 90 mph for those areas. The design wind speed for temporary structures in these area would therefore be 0.75 x 90 = 68 mph.

The draft standard also permits a reduction in windage area can be permitted, provided that such elements can be removed in less than 5 minutes and that the method of wind monitoring and removal of the equipment shall be clearly defined in the Operations Management Plan. Not withstanding the above, the darft standard requires that the structure shall be designed to resist wind forces on all elements associated with the design wind speed of 40mph.

Video Screens

The use of large video screens at outdoor sporting or other entertainment occasions has become increasingly popular. The requirement has resulted in a number of types of supporting structure being developed. Essentially, there are two distinct methods of supporting the screen so that the wind forces can be safely resisted. The actual method chosen is generally dependant on the construction of the screen modules themselves.

Some screen modules are designed so that they can be 'flown' – that is to say that there construction allows a number of modules to be hung from each other. The top row of modules is attached to a lifting truss or beam and the other modules are hung below. The modules usually connect to each other precisely and with a tight tolerance. It is therefore important to ensure that the lifting beam or truss is sufficiently stiff so there is little deflection under load. If this is not the case then it would be difficult to rig the screen correctly so that there are no gaps between the modules which would detract from the quality of the overall picture.

The lifting beam or truss is raised and lowered on a ground support structure. This structure is required to both support the weight of the screen and resist the horizontal forces from the wind. This structure could be a 'goal post' with braces to the towers to transfer the horizontal wind forces down to ground level. The weight of the screen is substantial and is used to 'ballast' the structure to resist overturning.

It is important to determine if the client wishes to apply 'branding' or other banners to the structure before the design is commenced as the wind forces on such items can be substantial. If stability cannot be achieved in high winds when the banners are attached, then the allowable wind speed is determined when the factor of safety against overturning is at an acceptable level. The operating manuals or structural calculations should state this wind speed and state that the banners should be removed at this wind speed.

Clearly, it is not possible to take the screen down quickly in event of extreme weather conditions and so emergency guy ropes are often supplied to ensure the structure remains safe even at very high wind speeds.

It is important that screen module manufacturer determines the allowable wind speed which a group of modules can resist without breaking up. The modules could be likened to a 'sail' presented to the wind. The structure can be designed to resist the forces associated with high

Mitsubishi video screen support structure

winds, but if the screen modules break up then the point has been missed. No need to have a extremely strong mast on a yacht if the sail cloth rips...

Other screen modules can be free standing and are stacked one above the other. The support structure is only therefore required to resist the horizontal wind forces. These are often referred to as back support structures. The actual design again depends on the attachment points which are available on the rear face of the modules. They comprise vertical ladder trusses which are attached to base beams. These ladders cantilever from the base beams and resist the lateral wind loads. They are therefore subjected to bending and as such the chords experience tension and compression depending on the direction of the wind. The compression chords must therefore be braced to prevent them from buckling laterally. This is often achieved by bracing them together with snap braces or similar.

It is important to ensure that the base beams are levelled very accurately so that the screen modules sit squarely and gaps between them do not develop as the modules are stacked to form the whole screen.

Consideration should be given to how to raise the modules safely. One possible solution is to attach davits to the top of the ladders. These davits support a runway beam which is provided with a trolley hoist to raise the modules into position. One disadvantage with this system is that the bottom of

Unitek structure showing 'branding' banners

the screen is close to the ground which can detract from the view of the screen from distance. Possible solutions to this problem include the provision of dummy modules at the bottom of the screen to raise the viewable area and also raising the whole structure above ground with a staging or decking system.

PA Towers and Delay Towers

The use of 'delay towers' in an outdoor environment is frequently a subject which is not given the due attention that it warrants. There have been a number of accidents where the structures have been blown over, causing serious injury in one particular instance in the UK. These structures are often positioned within the body of the audience and as such their stability must be of paramount importance.

Structures which specifically designed for the purpose should be used where possible. Equipment that was designed for load placement should not be used for load support. Clearly, the manufacturers' guidelines and recommendations must be followed at all times.

Wind forces on the speaker clusters can be significant. If these forces are applied at height, which is more often the case with delay towers than not, then the overturning moment on the tower can be relatively high. So, similar to the screen support structures, a structure is required which will support vertical loads whilst also being able to resist horizontal loads without becoming unstable and overturning.

SSE TeePee

This could be achieved using a tripod structure as developed for SSE Ltd and known as the TeePee.

Alternatively, a single tower could be used as shown on the front cover. However, care should be taken when analysing such structures and checks must be made on the combination of axial and bending forces in the tower, both during erection and in service, as well as checking the overall stability of the structure under wind loading.

This type of PA tower was developed by Total Fabrications in the UK in the late 1990s for the European tour of Eros Ramazzotti.

The 'base' of the tower comprises two trusses with integral screw jacks that are placed at 60 degrees to one another. the trusses meet at a special corner block and support a braced hinge. the tower is incrementally raised by a chain hoist at the rear of the hinge. Once at the correct angle, the tower is locked and the load taken off the motor. The PA is then raised to a position directly over the centroid of the equilateral triangular footprint of the base. The weight of the PA therefore becomes the ballast that provided stability of the whole system. Each tower is 15 metres high, was very fast to erect, was inclined at 14 degrees, is designed to carry 2000 kg V-DOSC PA system

PA towers for Eros Ramazzotti

and be stable in 60 mph winds.

These structures are frequently positioned within the audience and therefore adequate measures must be taken to ensure that the public cannot gain access to the towers. Climbing the towers may affect the overall stability and may overstress or overload certain elements of the structure.

Outdoor Ground Support

Ground support structures which were originally designed for indoor use are sometimes required to be used outdoors. If this is the case then additional load cases need to be considered and the overall stability checked. The windage area of equipment supported and the structural elements themselves must be calculated in order to determine the wind forces which the structure must be able to resist.

These horizontal forces are usually resisted by guy ropes which are attached at grid level. However, if the towers have sufficient axial and bending strength, then these guy ropes may not be required. Advice should be sought from the manufacturer regarding the use of such structures outdoors.

Ground Support used as a roof / sunshade, Israel

Management of Outdoor Structures

Let us now consider the on-site management of a structure where a maximum design wind speed has been specified and agreed with the client/ user. The management of the site is critical to its safety. To ensure the safe operation of facilities up to a maximum wind speed, requires continuous recording of the wind speed while persons are on or around the structure and also requires a management plan defining various procedures.

The design documentation which is supplied with the structure must clearly state the procedures and actions to be put in place if it is anticipated that the operational maximum wind speed will be exceeded. A notice should be clearly displayed on the structure and in the site office giving the wind speed at which various actions have to be taken and details of the actions required. The User should maintain a constant liaison with local weather centres and airports to determine if adverse weather conditions are expected in the area where the structure is erected.

It is important to note that anemometers should be positioned so that they give accurate readings of the wind speed and are not affected by air flows around the structure.

Anemometers should either be positioned some considerable distance away from all large obstructions so that the wind speeds should be measured in 'clean' air – avoiding turbulence and shelter from surrounding features and fixed to the structure itself. The Building Research Establishment (BRE) in the UK have suggested that the anemometer should be attached to a pole on top of the structure and suggest that the height of the pole should be 30% of the maximum height of the structure plus 1 metre.

The BRE also suggests that it would be prudent to have an audible and/or visual series of warnings to alert the on-site personnel of the status of the wind speed and to have a management plan of actions required at each warning level in accordance with the design documentation.

It is suggested that such plans should include three levels of warning to ensure that persons on or around the structure are not put at risk:

Level 1 - 70% of the wind load - staff briefed on their responsibilities and the possible actions required under the management plan.

Level 2 - 80% of the wind load - in conjunction with an increasing trend of recorded wind speeds, staff should be put on alert that action may be required.

Level 3 - 90% of the wind load - in conjunction with an increasing trend of recorded wind speeds, the operational procedures defined in the management plan should be implemented and the site secured against access by the public.

If an isolated gust speed is recorded in excess of the level 3 gust speed against a background of a generally falling level of wind speed, a further period of monitoring may be appropriate before implementation of the management plan.

It should be noted that these percentages refer to wind load and not wind speed and that the wind load is proportional to the square of the wind speed.

All wind speeds measured should be referenced at 10 metres above ground level. It is possible to generate a table of wind speeds for different height which give values of gust speeds at various heights for the level 1, 2 and 3 warnings.

The careful assessment of wind loads on structures at the design stage and, equally importantly, the on site management, monitoring of wind speeds and the implementation of derigging procedures are clearly critical if structures are to be used safely outdoors.

A typical example of an Operational Management Plan in the US would be as follows:

Operations Management Plan

Items to be included, but not necessarily limited to:
- Design wind criteria:
  - Basic design wind speed 90 mph, 3 sec gust in accordance with ASCE 7
  - Roof to be lowered to stage level at 60 mph, and skins removed
  - Sound cabinets to be lowered to stage level at 60 mph, 3 sec gust and laterally restrained
  - Scrims on sound wings to be removed at 40 mph, 3 sec gust
  - Scrim or back drop to be removed at 20 mph, 3 sec gust
  - Wind speeds are measured at 30 feet above ground level

- Other documentation
  This document shall be read in conjunction with the following documents
    - Operating Manual provided by Manufacturer
    - BSR E1.21 Entertainment Technology – Temporary Stage Roofs
    - Signed and sealed Engineering Report by Manufacturer / Engineer

- Monitoring
  - The wind speed shall be monitored and records shall be kept on site.
  - The wind speed measurements shall be taken at the height of the roof structure above ground, at a location where a true wind speed will be measured.
  - A competent, responsible person from Client will be present on site for the whole of the period of the installation.
  - A regular liaison with the local airports and weather information centres will be maintained to ascertain if any significant weather events are expected in the immediate vicinity of the roof structures.

- Pressures
    - It should be recognized that the pressure and wind loadings on a structures are proportional to the square of the wind speed

- Actions

    The following actions will be undertaken by Client personnel on site when the 3 second wind speed gusts approach the following speeds against a background of rising wind speeds
    - Backdrop
        - Level 1: 60% design wind load at 15.5 mph
          Personnel to be on alert
        - Level 2: 80% design wind load at 17.9 mph
          Personnel to be put on standby
          to remove the backdrop
        - Level 3: 100% design wind load at 20 mph
          Personnel to remove the backdrop
    - Sound wing scrims
        - Level 1: 60% design wind load at 31 mph
          Personnel to be on alert
        - Level 2: 80% design wind load at 35.8 mph
          Personnel to be put on standby
          to remove the scrims
        - Level 3: 100% design wind load at 40 mph
          Personnel to remove the scrims
    - Main roof grid
        - Level 1: 60% design wind load at 46.5 mph
          Personnel to be on alert
        - Level 2: 80% design wind load at 53.7 mph
          Personnel to be put on standby
          to lower the roof
        - Level 3: 100% design wind load at 60 mph
          Personnel to lower roof to stage
          level and remove skins
    - Main sound cabinets
        - Level 1: 60% design wind load at 46.5 mph
          Personnel to be on alert
        - Level 2: 80% design wind load at 53.7 mph
          Personnel to be put on standby
          to lower the sound cabinets
        - Level 3: 100% design wind load at 60 mph
          Personnel to lower the sound cabinets
          and restrain laterally

The following elements should also be considered when developing the Operations Management Plan for an event:
- Equipment on stage
- Evacuation of the site
- Closure of site to public
- The stage itself (wind can cause uplift on stage decks)
- Mixer tower
- Delay towers

Guy Ropes

The diagrams on the following pages show the layout of guy lines on a typical roof structure. Various manufacturers suggest slightly different arrangements, but all should allow the passage of lateral and vertical forces applied to the roof canopy to be safely transmitted and resisted at ground level to reduce or eliminate the bending moment in the towers.

However, a small number of companies offer roof structures which do not need guy wires as the towers are designed to withstand the bending moments associated with the application of lateral loads on the roof. The large roof supplied by Edwin Shirley Staging is a case in point. The towers have a considerable cross section - over a metre square - and are provided with a large amount of ballast at their bases. The disadvantage of such towers is that they are heavy and cannot be readily lifted manually and fork lifts or similar have to be used.

Roof structures are designed for a given wind speed which varies dependent on where in the world the structure is to be used. Typical mean design wind speeds for Total Fabrications' roof structures are between 18 to 34 metres per second which equates to 40 to 75 miles per hour. The concert will usually be cancelled when the wind speed reaches about forty miles an hour as it is difficult to hear the PA.

Clearly, the stability of the roof structure in adverse weather conditions is dependant on the adequacy of the guy ropes, and these can be secured in a number of ways. Generally we would recommend the use of proprietary ground anchors. Clearly, it is the responsibility of the User to check the site of the roof structure for underground services before the ground anchors are installed.

These devices are driven into the ground and a small pull out force is then applied to mobilise the tilting piece at the head. Ground anchors of this type are very common and should be readily available. The safe working pull-out loads are obviously very dependent on the type of soil conditions. The anchors shall be designed by a competent person with the appropriate factor of safety against failure. It is suggested that the anchors be designed to carry the safe working load of the guy rope with an appropriate factor of safety. The literature for ground anchors generally includes safe load tables for various soil types. It is clear that an assessment of the ground conditions is critical to the performance of such anchors.

If the roof is left assembled, then the guy wires and the ground anchors should be checked by the User before each show and at regular intervals between shows.

Roof Showing Guy Ropes

(Not to scale)

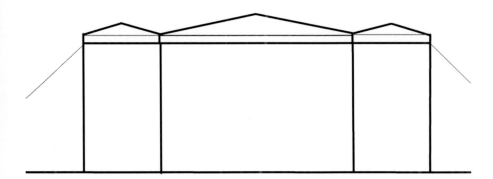

Front elevation showing PA wing

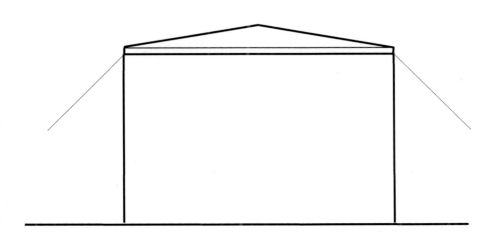

Back elevations (omitting PA wings for clarity)

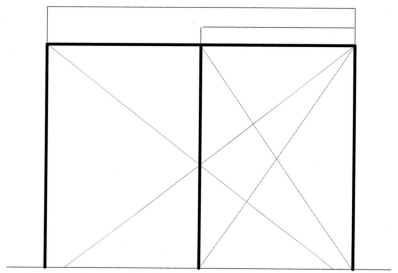

Side elevations showing cross bracing on side of main roof and on side of PA wing

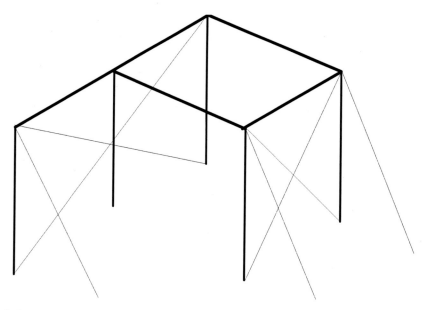

Angled view to show bracing on one side of roof and the PA wing

160 Aluminium Structures in the Entertainment Industry

It is also necessary to check the adequacy of the ground anchors when the moisture content of the ground changes significantly. As mentioned earlier, rain water pipes from the gutters should discharge well away from any tower bases, ground anchors and the like.

Water ballast or concrete blocks can be used in areas where ground anchors cannot be used. However, it should be appreciated that the allowable anchorage forces cannot be easily determined. For example, the force required to drag a large concrete weight on wet grass is going to be significantly different from that which is required to pull the same weight on gravel or tarmac. Each situation should be assessed by a competent person. You should be in no doubt that if the force in the guy ropes is say 2 tonnes, the weight of the concrete ballast or water ballast required is going to be significantly more than 2 tonnes, probably more like 5 or 6 tonnes.

The guy ropes which are crossed and stay within the footprint of the roof structure should also ideally be attached to the ground anchors.

Often users are tempted to attach the guy ropes to the bottom of the towers, thinking that there is sufficient vertical load in the tower to stop the bases slipping sideways. This is not usually the case. The lateral pull of the guy rope will dislodge the foot of the tower and may cause it to fall over, which could

Roof structure towers with guy wires and plan bracing

Ground anchor for guy wire

have disastrous consequences.

Users are also often tempted to attach the guy ropes to the stage. There is not generally enough dead weight in the stage to resist the upward loads. Usually the stage is also modular and hence the application of load at any one place will only be resisted by the dead weight of that area of the stage, which will be very small.

It would therefore be necessary to mobilise a large area of the stage by providing a structure to adequately join the modules together and provide ballast attached to the underside or supporting structure to the stage deck in order to resist the vertical loads from the guy ropes.

Let us now consider how much ballast is actually required to resist the horizontal loads at eaves level.

The amount of ballast required can be determined using the following procedures. It is assumed that there are no indentations or mechanical connection between the ballast and the ground and that overturning of the ballast is not critical. It is also assumed that the ground is level and that the roof is designed to support the vertical component of the tension in the guy rope, T cos a .

Local restraint to lateral forces may be transmitted by static friction between the contact surface of the ground and ballast. When the two are in contact and transmitting forces, there is a constant relationship between the

Coefficients of static friction are defined in Table 19 of BS 5975 Code of Practice for Falsework.

Minimum value of coefficient of static friction, μ					
Lower load accepting member	Upper load bearing member				
	Plain steel	Painted steel	Concrete	Softwood timber	Hardwood timber
Plain steel	0.15	0.1	0.1	0.2	0.1
Painted steel	0.1	0	0	0.2	0.2
Concrete	0.1	0	0.4	0.4	0.3
Softwood	0.2	0.2	0.4	0.4	0.3
Granular soil	0.3	0.3	0.4	0.3	0.3
Hardwood	0.1	0	0.3	0.3	0.1

value of the normal reaction and the force at which frictional lateral restraint is just overcome so that the ballast slides along the ground. This relationship is known as the coefficient of static friction.

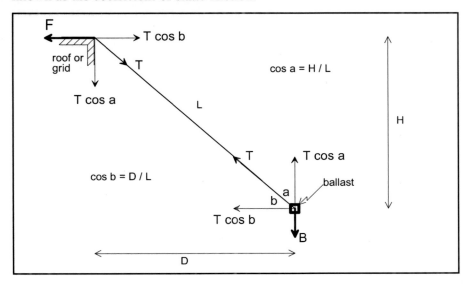

Where: F = force to be resisted
         a = angle between guy rope and vertical
         T = tension in the rope
         b = angle between guy rope and horizontal
         B = ballast required
         L = length of guy rope
         μ = coefficient of friction
         H = height of top fixing point of guy rope above ground
         FOS = factor of safety
         D = distance along ground from top fixing point of guy rope to
             ballast
         $\cos a = H / L$
         $\cos b = D / L$

Resolving horizontally at grid level

$$T . \cos b = F$$

$\therefore$ $F = T . \cos b$ or $T = F / \cos b$

The horizontal component of the tension in the guy rope, T cos b, must be resisted by friction between the ballast and the ground.

The vertical component of the tension in the guy rope, T cos a, must be subtracted from the weight of the ballast to find the net vertical force at the ballast.

The frictional force is the net vertical force multiplied by the coefficient of friction.

Assume a factor of safety, FOS against sliding

$$T . \cos b . FOS = (B - T . \cos a) . \mu$$

$\therefore$ $(F / \cos b). \cos b . FOS = (B - (F / \cos b) . \cos a) . \mu$

$\therefore$ $F . FOS = B . \mu - F . \dfrac{\cos a}{\cos b} . \mu$

$\therefore$ $F . FOS + F . \dfrac{\cos a}{\cos b} . \mu = B . \mu$

$$\therefore \quad B = \frac{F}{\mu} \cdot \left(FOS + \frac{\cos a}{\cos b} \cdot \mu \right)$$

$$\therefore \quad B = \frac{F}{\mu} \cdot \left(FOS + \frac{(H/L)}{(D/L)} \cdot \mu \right)$$

$$\therefore \quad B = \frac{F}{\mu} \cdot \left(FOS + \frac{H}{D} \cdot \mu \right)$$

For example:

If a concrete block is used as ballast and is placed on a concrete hard standing or on granular soil, then the coefficient of static friction is 0.4. Assume a factor of safety of 1.5.

Assume that the guy ropes reattached the edge of the roof 10 metres above ground and 12 metres along the ground from the edge of the roof.

Then substituting into the equation for the weight of ballast

$$B = \frac{F}{\mu} \cdot \left(FOS + \frac{H}{D} \cdot \mu \right)$$

$$B = \frac{F}{0.4} \, (1.5 + (0.83 \times 0.4))$$

$$B = 4.58 \, F$$

This shows that the weight of ballast required is 4.58 times the horizontal force at eaves level

Another example would be:

If a concrete block is used as ballast and is placed on a concrete hard standing or on granular soil, then the coefficient of static friction is 0.4. Assume a factor of safety of 1.5.

Assume that the guy ropes are attached the edge of the roof 12 metres above ground and 8 metres along the ground from the edge of the roof.

Then substituting into the equation for the weight of ballast

$$B = \frac{F}{\mu} \cdot \left(FOS + \frac{H}{D} \cdot \mu \right)$$

$$B = \frac{F}{0.4} \ (1.5 + (1.5 \times 0.4))$$

$$B = 5.25 \ F$$

This shows that the weight of ballast required is 5.25 times the horizontal force at eaves level.

Let us now consider the ballast required to resist a vertical load at eaves level:

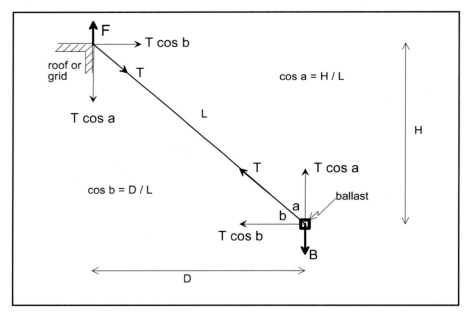

Where: F = force to be resisted
           a = angle between guy rope and vertical
           T = tension in the rope
           b = angle between guy rope and horizontal
           B = ballast required
           L = length of guy rope
           μ = coefficient of friction
           H = height of top fixing point of guy rope above ground
           FOS = factor of safety

D = distance along ground from top fixing point of guy rope to
   ballast

cos a = H / L

cos b = D / L

Resolving vertically at grid level

T . cos a = F

∴ F = T . cos a   or   T = F / cos a

The horizontal component of the tension in the guy rope, T cos b, must be resisted by friction between the ballast and the ground.

The vertical component of the tension in the guy rope, T cos a, must be subtracted from the weight of the ballast to find the net vertical force at the ballast.

The frictional force is the net vertical force multiplied by the coefficient of friction.

Assume a factor of safety, FOS against sliding

T . cos b . FOS = (B - T . cos a) . μ

∴ (F / cos a). cos b . FOS = (B - (F / cos a) . cos a) . μ

∴ F . FOS . $\dfrac{\cos b}{\cos a}$ = B . μ - F . μ

∴ F . FOS . $\dfrac{\cos b}{\cos a}$ + F . μ = B . μ

∴ B = $\dfrac{F}{μ}$. (FOS $\dfrac{\cos b}{\cos a}$ + μ)

∴ B = $\dfrac{F}{μ}$. (FOS . $\dfrac{(D / L)}{(H / L)}$ + μ)

$$\therefore \quad B = \frac{F}{\mu} \cdot (FOS \cdot \frac{D}{H} + \mu)$$

For example:

If a concrete block is used as ballast and is placed on a concrete hard standing or on granular soil, then the coefficient of static friction is 0.4. Assume a factor of safety of 1.5.

Assume that the guy ropes are attached the edge of the roof 10 metres above ground and 12 metres along the ground from the edge of the roof.

Then substituting into the equation for the weight of ballast

$$B = \frac{F}{\mu} \cdot (FOS \cdot \frac{D}{H} + \mu)$$

$$B = \frac{F}{0.4} ((1.5 \times 1.2) + 0.4))$$

$$B = 5.5\ F$$

This shows that the weight of ballast required is 5.5 times the vertical force at eaves level.

Another example would be:

If a concrete block is used as ballast and is placed on a concrete hardstanding or on granular soil, then the coefficient of static friction is 0.4. Assume a factor of safety of 1.5.

Assume that the guy ropes are attached to the edge of the roof 12 metres above ground and 8 metres along the ground from the edge of the roof.

Then substituting into the equation for the weight of ballast

$$B = \frac{F}{\mu} \cdot (FOS \cdot \frac{D}{H} + \mu)$$

$$B = \frac{F}{0.4} ((1.5 \times 0.66) + 0.4)$$

$$B = 3.48\ F$$

This shows that the weight of ballast required is 3.48 times the vertical force at eaves level.

Let us now consider the ballast required to resist a combination of vertical and horizontal forces at eaves level:

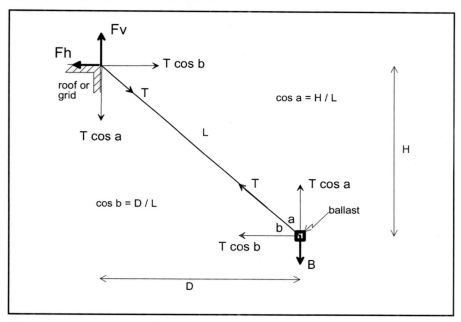

Where: Fv = vertical force to be resisted
          a = angle between guy rope and vertical
          Fh = horizontal force to be resisted
          T = tension in the rope
          b = angle between guy rope and horizontal
          B = ballast required
          L = length of guy rope
          μ = coefficient of friction
          H = height of top fixing point of guy rope above ground
          FOS = factor of safety
          D = distance along ground from top fixing point of guy rope to
              ballast
          cos a = H / L
          cos b = D / L

There will be a nett vertical force applied to the roof or grid. Therefore the resolution of T cannot be equated to Fh or Fv. Therefore split T into two components Tv, the tension in the rope to resist the vertical load and Th, the tension in the rope to resist the horizontal load.

$$T = Tv + Th$$

Resolving horizontally at grid level

$$Th \cdot \cos b = Fh$$

$$\therefore \quad Fh = Th \cdot \cos b \quad \text{or} \quad Th = Fh / \cos b$$

Resolving vertically at grid level

$$Tv \cdot \cos a = Fv$$

$$\therefore \quad Fv = Tv \cdot \cos a \quad \text{or} \quad Tv = Fv / \cos a$$

The horizontal component, of the tension in the guy rope, T cos b, must be resisted by friction between the ballast and the ground.

The vertical component of the tension in the guy rope, T cos a, must be subtracted from the weight of the ballast to find the net vertical force at the ballast.

The frictional force is the net vertical force multiplied by the coefficient of friction.

Assume a factor of safety, FOS against sliding.

Consider tension in rope, Th to resist horizontal force

$$Th \cdot \cos b \cdot FOS = (Bh - Th \cdot \cos a) \cdot \mu$$

$$\therefore \quad (Fh / \cos b) \cdot \cos b \cdot FOS = (Bh - (Fh / \cos b) \cdot \cos a) \cdot \mu$$

$$\therefore \quad Fh \cdot FOS = B \cdot \mu - Fh \cdot \frac{\cos a}{\cos b} \cdot \mu$$

$$\therefore \quad Fh \cdot FOS + Fh \cdot \frac{\cos a}{\cos b} \cdot \mu = Bh \cdot \mu$$

$$\therefore \quad Bh = \frac{Fh}{\mu} \cdot \left(FOS + \frac{\cos a}{\cos b} \cdot \mu \right)$$

$$\therefore \quad Bh = \frac{Fh}{\mu} \cdot \left(FOS + \frac{(H/L)}{(D/L)} \cdot \mu \right)$$

$$\therefore \quad Bh = \frac{Fh}{\mu} \cdot \left(FOS + \frac{H}{D} \cdot \mu \right)$$

Consider tension in rope, Tv to resist vertical force

$$Tv \cdot \cos b \cdot FOS = (Bv - Tv \cdot \cos a) \cdot \mu$$

$$\therefore \quad (Fv / \cos a) \cdot \cos b \cdot FOS = (Bv - (Fv / \cos a) \cdot \cos a) \cdot \mu$$

$$\therefore \quad Fv \cdot FOS \cdot \frac{\cos b}{\cos a} = Bv \cdot \mu - Fv \cdot \mu$$

$$\therefore \quad Fv \cdot FOS \cdot \frac{\cos b}{\cos a} + Fv \cdot \mu = Bv \cdot \mu$$

$$\therefore \quad Bv = \frac{Fv}{\mu} \cdot \left(FOS \cdot \frac{\cos b}{\cos a} + \mu \right)$$

$$\therefore \quad Bv = \frac{Fv}{\mu} \cdot \left(FOS \cdot \frac{(D/L)}{(H/L)} + \mu \right)$$

$$\therefore \quad Bv = \frac{Fv}{\mu} \cdot \left(FOS \cdot \frac{D}{H} + \mu \right)$$

The total weight of ballast B = Bh + Bv

$$B = \frac{Fh}{\mu} \cdot \left(FOS + \frac{H}{D} \cdot \mu \right) + \frac{Fv}{\mu} \cdot \left(FOS \cdot \frac{D}{H} + \mu \right)$$

Application of Payload

We talked earlier about tower stability theory. It would be worth going back to that subject and consider when the payload is applied to a roof top structure.

If the grid is raised off the ground by say a couple of metres, the towers extend vertically above the sleeve. The chain passes over the top of the head block and hence the load is applied at the top of the tower. Each tower is therefore a vertical cantilever and has an effective length of double its actual height. The allowable load on such a tower is considerably less than when the tower is fully or partially restrained at each end.

It should also be appreciated that the roof grid grid is unrestrained before it climbs the towers and the guy ropes are attached.

You should therefore check if the tower with $K = 2$ can carry the self weight of the roof grid plus the payload, with, of course, the 25% additional load due to snatch of the chain motor. The towers are, therefore, required to resist these loads in lateral bending. Clearly, the worst case scenario is when the grid is at trim height before the guy ropes are attached. It is usual for the manufacturer to define the maximum allowable wind speed that the roof structure should be exposed to without guy wires. This is typically a small fraction of the full design wind speed.

If these conditions are not met, then it will be necessary to raise the roof grid to trim height before applying the payload.

You should also check if the motor itself will give sufficient lift, i.e. half the total load on the tower. If not, then you will need to consider lifting the grid to trim height and locking off the grid to the towers before adding the payload.

We should consider what would happen if there an electrical fault with the motors or the lighting or sound equipment. As with all systems of this nature, adequate grounding should be provided.

Earthing

Aluminium is a very good conductor of electricity. In fact the electrical conductivity is about four times that of steel. Earthing or grounding of an aluminium structure can therefore be easily achieved. However, it should be noted that there is not a proper electrical connection between the main roof structure or ground support grid structure and the towers as the structure is guided up and down the towers with nylon wheels in the sleeve blocks. Therefore a suitable earth bond should be provided between each tower and the roof or grid structure.

I would suggest that an adequate number of earth rods be positioned in the ground and be connected to earth clamps on the roof structure itself by suitable wiring. The surface of the aluminium should be cleaned with wire wool to remove the oxidisation on the surface of the aluminium before the earth clamps are fitted in order to get a good electrical contact.

As the structures usually carry a number of electrical items, all indoor and outdoor structures should be properly earthed to reduce the risk of electrocution.

Overturning

A number of people advocate that the scaffold towers are stable up to a height of three times the base dimension. This cannot be accepted without qualification. For example, scaffold towers are sometimes used as a means to support PA on either side of the main stage or as delay towers within the audience. The effect of wind loading on the stability has to be carefully considered. If the PA is located at one side of the tower and the wind blows from opposite side, then the tower may become unstable or even overturn depending on the force of the wind, the height of the PA above the ground and the area of the PA which is subjected to wind loading.

The tower will overturn when the overturning moment is greater than the restoring moment. As discussed earlier, the recommended factor of safety against overturning should be taken as 1.5 in accordance with 'Temporary Demountable Structures' as published by the IStructE.

The same argument is valid for four tower ground support systems. If the PA is 'flown' from the front truss, then there system may become unstable with winds from the rear.

There are two obvious solutions to the problem of overturning. Firstly, one could provide guy ropes and ballast/ground anchors to resist the horizontal wind forces. Secondly, one could determine the wind speed at which the factor of safety against overturning is 1.5. The PA should be lowered to the ground when the wind speed approaches this wind speed. This could well result in an unrealistically low allowable wind speed, in which case other solutions will need to be considered.

13 STAGES

Normally, a stage area is provided beneath a ground support or an outdoor roof structure, to elevate the performers above the spectators. There are a number of proprietary stage systems on the market today.

But what is a typical temporary outdoor stage? These are generally of lightweight modular construction and are constructed from steel or aluminium frames supporting plywood decks that are generally painted matt black. The typical size of the deck units is two metres by one metre or eight feet by four feet. Half-sized units are also often supplied. The decks are supported by a modular substructure, such as system scaffolding or a proprietary matrix of ladder trusses, link beams and node posts. The deck units sometimes lock to the adjacent deck units and sometimes are mechanically fixed to the substructure. However, frequently the deck units are placed individually on the framework below, without any mechanical fixings, relying on gravity to hold them in place.

The design loading on stages is dependent on the use. British Standard 6399 Loadings for Buildings states that a stage in a public assembly area where the stage is susceptible to overcrowding should be designed for a superimposed load of 7.5 kN/m^2 (153 lbs/ft^2) or a point load of 4.5 kN (1011 lbs) over area of 50 mm by 50 mm. The document also states that stages in areas of possible physical activities should be designed for 5 kN/m^2 (102 lbs/ft^2) or a point load of 3.6 kN (809 lbs).

American design standards are slightly different from those published in the UK. ASCE 7 indicates that the uniformly distributed load should be 100 lbs/ft^2 (4.79 kN/m^2) with no stipulation for concentrated loads. On the other hand, the 1997 Uniform Building Code states that stage areas should be designed for 125 lbs/ft^2 (6.125 kN/m^2).

So, we have some disagreement between various standards. It has been argued that the design load should be increased to 7.5 kN/m^2 (153 psf) if there is a significant risk of stage invasion. In summary, we are usually designing for a vertical load between 4.88 kN/m^2 (100 psf) and 7.5 kN/m^2 (153 psf).

It is important to consider the deflection of the stage deck units when they are under load. If one unit is heavily loaded and the adjacent one is not, then

A wooden stage structure typical of Far Eastern construction

the deflection of the loaded unit could cause a tripping hazard. So the support framework for the plywood decking needs to be sufficiently stiff to limit the deflection differential. Alternatively, the deck units could be bolted together.

Stages need to be adequately braced to resist the horizontal loads which are induced by the sway forces. There has been great deal of discussion in the UK about the value of these forces. The current consensus is that the stage should be able to withstand a vertical load of 5 kN/m² and a simultaneous horizontal force of 5% of this value, applied in one horizontal direction at the surface of the stage.

The ASCE and UBC documents do not specifically require sway to be considered. However, it is common engineering practice to design a structure to resist horizontal sway loads acting in two orthogonal directions. These are separate load cases and need not be considered simultaneously. *Temporary Demountable Structures* states that these sway loads should be assumed to be 5% of the vertical design load and should be applied at stage level.

Let us consider an example to put this into perspective. Imagine a 60 foot x 40 foot stage (a fairly common size) with a design load of 100 lbs/ft², so the total vertical design load is approximately 240,000 pounds – in excess of 108 tonnes. The lateral sway force would be 5% of this, which is 12,000 pounds in excess of 5 tonnes - a significant force The need for substantial bracing now becomes clear.

If the stage is a relatively low height, then it may be possible to show that the horizontal sway loads can be resisted by the support posts in bending, rather like a regular ground support system or table, provided that there is a full moment connection at the top of the leg and not just a pin joint. However, if the stage is raised to three feet or over, then lateral bracing will probably be required in both directions.

In the Far East, stages are often constructed on site from timber It is unlikely that such stages would comply with 'western' design standards.

Usually, there is a sterile area in front of the stage which is protected by a front stage barrier. This prevents the crowd from reaching the front of the stage. In this case the stage would normally be designed for a vertical load of 5 kN/m^2 with a horizontal load of 5% of the vertical load applied at the level of the stage.

The dynamic response of stages to loads is a complicated subject. The response of the stage depends on the stiffness and mass of the stage and, of course, the frequency of the applied load. This subject can be case sensitive and you should seek specialist advice before proceeding with any stage structure which involves synchronised dynamic loading caused by such activities as dancing and jumping.

Guidance is provided in Annex A of BS 6399. This document suggests that "Vertical jumping also generates a horizontal load which may be critical for some structures e.g. temporary grandstands. A horizontal load of 10% of the vertical load should be considered."

'Temporary Demountable Structures' as published by the IStructE gives more data on the design loads of stage structures.

One issue that is often overlooked is the design of the stage structure if a crowd barrier is not provided. If the crowd surges forward, then the stage needs to be able to resist the horizontal crowd loading. That is, if there is no crowd barrier, then the designer needs to consider the possible force from the crowd pushing against the edge of the stage. In the U.K. this is assumed to be 3 kN/m run x factor of 1.5 at a height of 1.1 meters above the ground = 4.5 kN/m run. This is equivalent to 308 plf at 3' 6" above the ground and would amount to 18,500 pounds along the front of a 60 foot wide stage. Clearly, this load is in addition to the sway force discussed earlier. Clearly, the front of the stage would need to be designed as a handrail with the rails being at suitable heights and have no sharp edges or points and the area below the stage should be adequately screened off to prevent tampering.

These above mentioned forces are usually considered in stage design, but wind uplift on stage decks is something that is not. Wind uplift is a design case that until now has been overlooked by many designers and engineers. Whilst this issue is not expressly catered for in design codes in the UK, it is a situation which should be considered in the design and use of temporary outdoor stages.

The analysis of wind loading on a fixed building is a complex subject and is generally undertaken on a case specific basis. The analysis would consider a multitude of factors, including the geographical location of the building, the terrain, the proximity of neighboring buildings, the building's roof profile, the shape of the building in plan, and the height of the building, to name but a few factors. Now engineers are faced with a problem: What parameters should one use to determine the wind forces on a stage structure that could be used in numerous locations, orientations, sizes, and so on?

A recent failure of a temporary stage has prompted a flurry of legal action and standards work in the U.K. High winds had caused a number of the stage's deck units to lift off the substructure and blow across the site. One person was hit by a flying deck unit and was very badly hurt.

The incident resulted in legal action involving the Health and Safety Executive (similar to OSHA in the U.S.). To help prevent this from happening again, the Building Research Establishment in the U.K. has issued a draft document offering guidance on the design of temporary outdoor stages against wind uplift. This document is being considered by the Advisory Group on Temporary Structures, which is part of the Institution of Structural Engineers in the U.K., and its provisions may be written into the ISE's guidance document, *Temporary Demountable Structures: Guidance on Design, Procurement and Use.*

Lighting or sound equipment or perhaps flight cases are often stored under the stage and form obstructions to the flow of air. As the wind hits these obstructions a net vertical pressure is induced on the underside of the deck which results in additional uplift forces.

In the U.K. there have been conflicting opinions on how to analyze the possible uplift forces on a stage deck. However, it has now been accepted that the stage should be considered as a flat canopy roof with or without open sides, depending on whether the stage has a facing that goes to the ground or whether sufficient equipment is stored under the stage to disrupt the flow of the wind. Pressure coefficients for the areas of a flat roof are widely known, and it is appreciated that higher values occur around the edges. These pressure coefficients are multiplied by the basic wind pressure that is derived from the wind speed and other factors to give an uplift force on a deck. The self weight of the deck unit is then compared to the uplift force to give the factor of safety against uplift. Let us consider an extremely simple example.

The basic wind load formula in the Uniform Building Code is

$$P = C_e \times C_q \times q_s \times I_w$$

where
P = design wind pressure
C_e = combined height, exposure and gust factor
C_q = pressure coefficient for the structure
q_s = wind stagnation pressure = $0.00256 \times V_e^2$
where V_e = effective wind speed
I_w = importance factor

Rearranging the formula

$$q_s = P / (C_e \times C_q \times I_w)$$
$$V_e = (P / 0.00256 \; C_e \times C_q \times I_w)^{0.5}$$

If we assume that the maximum local pressure coefficient for a mono-pitch canopy with side walls occurs in the area around the edge, $C_q = 2.3$ outward. The combined height, exposure and gust factor, $C_e = 1.06$ for a structure with Exposure C and height above the ground of less than 15 feet.

When one applies this formula with these coefficients and an importance factor, $I_w = 1.0$, it is possible to compile a table of the self-weight of a deck against the wind speed to lift the deck.

Deck weight psf	Deck weight kg/m2	Wind speed mph	Wind speed m/s
2	10	17.9	8.0
3	15	21.9	9.8
4	20	25.3	11.3
5	25	28.3	12.9
6	30	31.0	13.9

We can do a similar exercise for a mono pitch canopy without side walls, that is to say a stage with open sides. The maximum local pressure coefficient around the edge of the stage would be reduced to C_q = 1.7 outward. The figures, assuming that the other parameters remain the same, then become

Deck weight psf	Deck weight kg/m2	Wind speed mph	Wind speed m/s
2	10	23.3	10.4
3	15	28.6	12.8
4	20	33.0	14.7
5	25	36.9	16.5
6	30	40.4	18.1

After looking at these wind speeds, one may ask why we haven't heard a catalog of failures. It must be appreciated that this is a very simplistic approach and doesn't cover all eventualities. Various factors affect the uplift forces and these include friction or continuity between the adjacent decks, friction between the decks and the substructure, the amount of blockage under the stage, the edge detail, height of the stage, the proximity of obstructions around the stage, terrain, et cetera. It should also be appreciated that the pressure coefficient towards the center of the stage will be significantly less that that around the perimeter. Therefore, if the edge decks are restrained, the allowable wind speed for the stage as a whole will be higher. Furthermore, if the side walls are taken away, then the wind can travel under the stage and the pressure coefficient will be reduced, which also will increase the allowable wind speed.

The wind speeds shown in the table are quite low compared with the design wind speed for the roof above the stage, which is typically 70 mph. So what can be done to increase the wind speed at which the decks become unstable? One obvious solution is to add weight to the deck units, particularly those around the perimeter of the stage. If weights are placed on top of the decks, then care should be taken to ensure that these weights themselves cannot be blown away. Another possible solution is to hang weights under the deck units, but this may not be practical. Relying on the weight of rostra and similar equipment also should be treated with caution; someone may not appreciate their function as ballast and move them out of the way.

It has been suggested that the deck units could be mechanically fixed to the substructure. However, care should be taken with this approach as the substructure is generally a lightweight modular system, which could weigh less than 10 kg/m^2 (2 psf). Therefore using the substructure as ballast would not have a significant effect on the wind speed at which the deck units become unstable. Porous decks could be considered, but these would not normally be acceptable to the touring concert market. In fact, porous decks may be more of liability than a benefit if they increase the risks of tripping to performers and other workers.

The decks around the perimeter are at the greatest risk of instability especially from vortices which may be set up due disturbances in the air flow. Particular attention should be paid to these areas of the stage in periods of adverse weather conditions.

It is therefore important that the designer states clearly in the manual for the stage structure the operating limits with particular reference to the maximum allowable wind speed and the effect of obstructions under the stage decks.

In any case, designers need to consider wind effects on outdoor stages as well as on overhead stage roofs, and take steps to guard against flying deck units. Designers need to use their heads to keep their feet on the ground!

14 USER INFORMATION AND INSPECTIONS

Regular inspections of structures are an important part of engineering. A multi-storey car park in England partially collapsed in 1997 and there have been calls for all such structures to be inspected by Structural Engineers on an annual basis. Most major bridges are the subject of major inspections as are masts and towers.

Aluminium structures in the entertainment industry are quite different to other structures in many ways. They are frequently made up from a kit of standard parts and often are transported from venue to venue during a tour. They are therefore subjected to considerable wear and tear in their life-time.

An upright empty beer can will usually carry the weight of a small person. However, if the same can is dented and the same person stands on it again, it will usually collapse. So we can see that the axial load capacity of the beer can is substantially reduced when it has been damaged.

The chords of the trusses are usually circular tubular members, not dissimilar in diameter to a beer can, but of thicker gauge. If the chord is damaged in a similar way to the beer can, then it will probably be unable to carry the original design loads. We can therefore quickly see that regular and frequent inspections are necessary to ensure that structures in the entertainment industry continue to perform as originally intended.

Operating Manuals are provided by reputable manufacturers and are available to customers, potential customers and others who may be interested in reading them. They are imaginatively entitled 'Operating Manual for Modular Aluminium Truss and Tower Sections Designed and Fabricated by Total Fabrications Ltd' and also the 'Operating Manual for Demountable Aluminum Roof Top Structures Designed and Fabricated by Total Fabrications Limited'.

The purpose of these manuals is to assist the people who purchase our products to use them safely, and the same is applicable to all major manufacturers

The manuals cover a range of topics and describe the materials used, the application of loads, wind forces on roofs, maximum and minimum payloads, use of spansets and round slings, connections, ground anchors on roofs, towers and stabilisers, ground bearing capacity, supervision of the erection and dismantling of the structure, grounding or earthing, chains and hoists, tower lifting frames, roof covers, transportation, handling and erection, care and storage, inspection of the components by the user and when the equipment should be taken out of service.

The labels which are now used by reputable manufacturers have Serial Numbers which enable them to keep records of the date of manufacture, the purchaser, etc.

If the User is a rental company and has a large stock of trusses, then he should consider introducing a procedure of tracking his stock. Clearly, if he has a large warehouse full of truss products, then there could be a tendency to use the truss which is closest to the entrance doors first. When the equipment is returned, it will again be placed near to the entrance doors. The next rental is agreed and the same truss is used again. Obviously some sections of the truss are then used much more extensively than others, and will have a much shorter life as a result.

The owner of the product should consider marking each truss, tower section, base, head block or whatever with an individual number or bar code. He should then consider setting up a database to keep a log of where each section of truss has been used, what loads it has carried, details of the user, record any damage (however minor), details of any remedial work etc, and so on. The Serial Numbers on the labels which are now used should facilitate this process.

This brings us neatly on to User Inspection. The user/owner should be aware that aluminium truss and tower sections do have a finite life and will not last forever.

However, it is very difficult to quantify the design life of aluminium trusses. A manufacturer is not able to determine the level of usage of the product, the care with which it will be used, the loads to which it will be subjected, and all these factors have a significant effect on the life of the product.

For example, if a piece of truss is used every day and is loaded up to its full capacity, then it will in all probability have a shorter life span than a comparable piece of truss which is used once a month and only loaded to half its capacity on each use. So we can see that fatigue of the structures and the design life of the various elements are difficult to assess.

The typical curves which are published for various types of aluminium alloy show that fatigue strength varies considerably from alloy to alloy. Typically 6082-T6 reduces its strength by some 50% after 100 million cycles. The specimen is subjected to what is known as a rotating cantilever test which involves the item being alternately loaded and unloaded – the load being such as to induce a high stress.

The reduction in strength is not significant until 100,000 cycles have been undertaken. Fatigue is therefore rarely a problem in the entertainment industry as the element would have to be fully loaded and unloaded twice a day for 136 years for the strength reduction became significant.

However, one should not discount the effects of fatigue on trusses and towers which are badly packed and then transported. It is difficult to assess or quantify what effects this could have, but one could conclude that it must be detrimental to the performance of the truss or tower.

The Working Group writing the ESTA/ANSI standard considered these issues very carefully. We finally agreed that manufacturers should give some guidance to owners and users on the inspection of equipment.

These procedures are set out in ANSI E1.2 standard, BS 7906 Part 2 and Temporary Demountable Structures. Similar procedures should also be set out in the operating manuals provided by manufacturer.

Let us consider the provision set out in these documents. It should be recognised by the user that a section of truss has a finite life span, dependant on use, handling and care. If the truss is subjected to damage, then the allowable loads will reduce, depending on the extent, location and type of damage. The truss should therefore be inspected to determine if any damage has occurred which would be detrimental to the performance of the truss.

The regular and proper inspection of the truss is the responsibility of the user and *not* the manufacturer. The user may wish to obtain advice from a chartered structural engineer, or other competent person, who has adequate experience in the use of structures of this type. It is he who will specify the type of testing and the acceptance levels.

The user shall undertake a thorough inspection of the truss on receipt from the manufacturer to determine if any damage has occurred in transit. If the truss is bought second-hand then the user shall undertake a full inspection of the equipment, including non-destructive testing.

The truss shall be inspected visually by the user before each use. If any significant damage to the truss elements or the welds is noted, then the section of truss shall <u>not</u> be used, and it should be clearly marked as such. As markings can be removed, the truss could re-enter the stock to be used. Therefore, consideration should be given by the user to removing the end plates or another similar action to render the truss section unusable.

The user shall undertake non destructive testing of the truss sections on a regular basis. The frequency of the testing is dependant on a number of factors, such as frequency of use, regular use of high payloads, method of transportation and the like.

It is suggested that the inspection procedures for truss in regular use shall be placed in two categories:

> Frequent inspection - visual inspection
> Periodic inspection - thorough inspection with non destructive testing.

As a minimum, the methods, extent and acceptance levels for non destructive testing of welded joints shall be in accordance with BS 8118. The Structural Use of Aluminium : Part 2 : Appendix B. Acceptance levels will be as defined by Table B.2 in Appendix B. It is expected that the tests would be conducted on a random sample of welds and that they would entail non destructive dye penetrant testing to show the location and extent of any fractures in the welds. Should any joint or weld be found to be unacceptable then the sample will be doubled in size and further tests carried out.

It should be noted that short minor hairline crater cracks at the start and stop positions of the weld run are to be expected. Propagation of these cracks should not occur.

The structural engineer acting on behalf of the user shall determine whether the results of the tests are acceptable, and his determination shall be final. On no account shall sections of truss be used where the welds have been found to be unacceptable.

For truss which is not in regular use, a suggested testing programme before re-use would be as follows:

> idle for 1 month or more - shall undergo frequent inspection.
> idle for 1 year or more - shall undergo periodic inspection.

For truss which is part of a permanent installation, a suggested testing programme would be as follows:

> if stationary - shall undergo periodic inspection, the frequency of which will depend upon exposure and percentage of allowable load which is applied.

if part of a moving system - shall undergo periodic testing every 3
months.

Inspection records shall be kept by the owner for each section of truss and tower. The records shall include reference to the serial number and shall be dated and signed by the person conducting the inspection. The documents should also include recommendations of when trusses should be taken out of service. It is worth considering each of these items in turn.

The specification of the allowable level of damage which can be tolerated by a section of truss before the load carrying capacity is significantly affected is a complex issue. The structural calculations for the particular truss determine the most critical member or connection in a run of truss. Clearly, if this critical member (or connection) is damaged it will have a greater impact on the allowable load-carrying capacity of the truss than if a non-critical member was damaged. If a non critical member (or connection) is damaged then the resulting loss of strength may render this member (or connection) as critical to the load-carrying capacity of the truss.

If the user is unclear on the level of damage which is unacceptable, then he should contact the relevant manufacturer.

As a general rule, truss sections shall not be used when any of the following are noted, and this list should not be considered as exhaustive.

a)   **General**
Cracked, partial complete or missing welds.
Significant wear to welds due to abrasion.
Unauthorised repairs by welding or other heat treatment.
Any modifications or repairs to truss which are not confirmed
acceptable in writing by the manufacturer.

b)   **Main chords, diagonals and secondary members**
Significant reduction in cross sectional area of member due to abrasion
Significant permanent deformation of the tube due to dents, lateral
    compression or the like.
Cracks or holes in the members (except drillings for connections and
    pressure relief during the manufacturing process).
Damaged or missing members.
Significant local or global bending of the member.

c) **Connections**

Significant deformation or elongation of the bolt or fixing holes in either the plates or the chords or the fork end connectors.

Corrosion at the interface of dissimilar metals. e.g. roll pin locations, bolts, connections.

Missing roll pins at connection.

Significant permanent deformation of the end plates of the truss (where applicable).

Damage to the end plates (where applicable).

When any of the above are noted, the truss should be clearly marked and shall not be used. As markings can be removed, the truss could re-enter the stock to be used, therefore, consideration should be given by the user to removing the end plates or similar to render the damaged truss section unusable.

If bolts, nuts or washers or other forms of connector are found to be defective then they should be immediately taken out of service and replaced with new. In any event, they should be replaced every 25 uses as a minimum. The user shall seek advice from the manufacturer of the connections if in any doubt about when they should be replaced.

The documents also include information and comments regarding maintenance of the truss or tower sections.

If the user undertakes maintenance work on sections of truss, such as the replacement of welds or structural elements, then the manufacturer cannot be held responsible for the future use or performance of the truss. The user shall be clear that the replacement of welds or structural elements by the user shall invalidate the load charts and structural calculations and any manufacturer's warranty.

If maintenance work is required on a section or sections of truss, then advice and approval shall be sought from the manufacturer.

Clearly, if the user does undertake remedial work to the sections where they are damaged then the responsibility for the future use of those sections is his. The manufacturer has no control over such remedial work and therefore cannot be held responsible for the performance of the truss or tower after any such work is done.

It should also be borne in mind that any damage should be assessed by a competent person who is experienced in dealing with problems of this kind, and it is his decision that should be final. He should be aware that damage to part of the truss may be an indication of damage on a larger scale which cannot necessarily be seen. For example, if a chord is buckled locally, then this may suggest that the truss has been overloaded – in which case, other damage may not be visible (such as overstressing) and the truss should be scrapped. This assessment of damage is a matter for 'engineering judgement'.

Truss and tower sections can suffer considerable damage in transit from one location to another, and it is the responsibility of the user or owner to ensure that the sections are packed so that they do not suffer from excessive abrasion during transportation. Consideration should be given to wrapping the truss or placing soft packers between the trusses.

The trusses should also be packed in a way that they are not overstressed during transportation. This means that they are not packed or stacked so as to place an undue load on any element of any adjacent truss.

Operating Manuals should also include comments about handling and erection and it is worth considering each of these areas in turn.

The trusses shall be handled so that significant abrasion and hence loss of metal does not occur. The truss shall be used in lengths which are defined in the structural calculations. It may be possible to use longer runs of truss with intermediate support positions but consideration should be given to movement joints to allow for secondary effects such as thermal expansion.

The truss shall be supported by load straps and round slings which are positioned at nodes on the trusses, sleeves and tower sections as appropriate. The supporting straps or round slings should be of sufficient dimensions that the transfer of load does not damage the truss locally i.e. steel wires should not be used as these could dig into the aluminium members (also see above).

The load straps or round slings must be installed in a way that they do not impose significant horizontal loads on the elements of the truss. It is the responsibility of the user to ensure that the truss is rigged correctly.

On no account shall trusses be dragged across the floor as this could lead to abrasion of the chords, which would result in loss of metal, or significant cuts, gouges or other damage which could result in stress concentrations and ultimately to stress fracturing.

Particular care should be taken when fork lifts are used to move truss sections. The positioning of the forks must never interfere with the diagonals in the truss section. Careful consideration shall be given to the induced bending and shear forces if a loaded truss is moved by fork lifts or similar. The bending moments and shear forces must be calculated for the given loading when the truss is supported by fork lifts and compared with those allowable. Consideration shall also be given to ensure that the chords are not subjected to undue local bending where the forks are positioned away from node points.

Clearly, inexperienced personnel should not be used and I would recommend that competent and experienced riggers be used on all projects, however small.

After the truss and tower sections are returned to the warehouse or other storage location, they should not be packed or stacked so that do not place undue load on any element of any adjacent truss. They should not be stored outside as this will cause unsightly surface corrosion of the aluminium and, in aggressive conditions, will reduce its design life.

Operating Manuals may also provide specific information regarding the setting up or erection of the structure.

This following is taken from the Operating Manual for Trusses and Towers which describes the setting up of a ground support system. It is worth considering each of these items in turn.

A ground support system is used where insufficient or inadequate 'flying' points are available in an indoor venue. Where a ground support system is used outdoors, consideration must be given to other types of loading such as wind loading.

The principle of ground support is that the tower passes through a sleeve section which is mechanically fixed to the truss. The configuration of the trusses is critical to the stability of the system as a whole. For example, a four-tower system has different characteristics to a two-tower or 'goal post' arrangement.

The system works by utilising the moment carrying connection between the sleeve and the tower, rather like a table.

The towers are normally raised and the grid set up at ground level and the grid lifted by way of chains which pass over the head pulley block and back down to the motor. The motor and the end of the chain are mechanically attached to the sleeve or the truss. Care must be taken when attaching the hook and motor to the sleeve or truss. The load straps or round slings shall be installed so that they do not impose significant horizontal loads on the elements of the truss or induce local bending of elements of the truss by positioning them between node points. It is the responsibility of the user to ensure that the truss is rigged correctly.

The bases of the towers are normally provided with outriggers to generate

Roof structure showing towers with outriggers and braces.

some level of base fixity. The combination of the base fixity and the moment carrying capacity of the sleeve provide stability for the system.

It is essential that the towers are vertical and that the truss is level during lifting and at trim height or final working position.

When the towers are free standing before the lift of the grid has commenced, they effectively cantilever above the sleeves. The effective length of the tower is therefore much greater at this stage than when the grid is at trim height. Consideration must therefore be given to lifting the grid to trim height before it is loaded if the capacity of the tower is insufficient when considered as a cantilever. It should be noted that the capacity of the tower is significantly less when it is considered to be an axially loaded cantilever than when it is considered to be restrained in direction and position at its base (when the stabilisers are fitted) and fixed in direction (but not position) by the sleeve block at the head of the tower. If the tower extends past the trim height of the grid, then the tower must be checked for buckling both above and below the grid.

Typical Tower with headblock and sleeve

A ground support system is best used where the site is level and the ground is firm. The foundation of the tower must be such that the tower will not settle when loaded. It is not possible to give precise advice on the size and type of foundation as ground conditions vary considerably. The user should seek advice from a suitably qualified person regarding the design of the footing for the base for the tower.

After the base locations have been established, the tower hinges are bolted to the base and the sleeves passed over the tower hinges. The grid is then assembled at ground level and bolted to the sleeves. The towers are assembled with the head blocks on the grid and raised into position using the tower lifting frame. The chains are passed over the head pulley blocks and the motor and chains are attached to the sleeve and grid structure.

The motors should be carefully calibrated so that they run at equal speeds so that loads are not shed from the slower motors. The grid is then raised up to a level where the stabilisers and stabiliser braces can be attached.

All the screw jacks should be adjusted so that they take load. Care should be taken to ensure that the screw jacks do not lift the base of the tower. The screw jacks can be used to ensure that the tower is vertical and some slackening and subsequent tightening of the clamps of the stabilisers may be required. The screw jacks should not be used so that an excessive amount of thread is visible below the stabiliser members and to this end additional packers may be required.

After the user is confident that all the towers are vertical the grid can be raised. Personnel should be positioned at each of the towers to check on the progress of the sleeve up the tower, to ensure that the chain is not twisted and to ensure that motor feed cable does not become snagged or damaged. The raising of the grid should be undertaken in stages to allow for adjustment for unequal motor travel and so ensure that the grid is horizontal during its travel up the towers.

The stabilisers at the foot of the tower can be very helpful when trying to make the tower vertical or plumb. As the screw jack is a considerable distance away from the foot of the tower, a small application of force at the screw jack position will push the tower. By adjusting the screw jacks at each of the four stabiliser positions, it is possible to 'fine tune' the verticality of the tower.

It is important to note that the stabilisers are not designed to take the vertical load of the tower, only to increase the stability. The screw jacks in the base should be adjusted so that they are all in contact with the ground and all carry approximately the same vertical load. This is easily achieved by turning each of them in turn and checking that they all show approximately the same level of resistance.

Other procedures may also be set out in the Operating Manuals.

The following is taken from the 'Operating Manual for Roof Top Structures' which describes the setting up of a roof top system. Again, it is worth considering each of these items in turn.

The same comments about the use of stabilisers to plumb the towers applies equally to roof structures as ground support structures, and the same comments regarding the ground under ground support towers apply to roof structures as well. The towers shall be founded on suitable bearing strata. The bearing pressure on the ground can be derived from the axial load of the tower in service and the area of the bearing plates. The allowable bearing pressures should be established on site and agreed with the Local and Statutory Authorities. Adequate spreader plates shall be used under the tower bases and also the stabiliser screw jacks, as appropriate.

Care should be taken when positioning rainwater pipes. They should be located away from the tower bases as changes in moisture content in the ground will change the allowable bearing capacity. With roof top structures it is particularly important to place the rain water pipes from the cover and well away from the tower bases and walkways.

15 SAFETY ISSUES

Some general matters of safety are discussed below, but these should not be considered as an exhaustive list and the User shall satisfy himself that all reasonable steps are taken to ensure the safety of the personnel who are erecting, operating and dismantling the system. Matters of safety should be the concern of all of us from conception, through design, engineering and manufacture to use.

Structures should only be used where they have been designed specifically for the purpose. For example, it is very important not to use proprietary equipment which was designed for use indoors in an outdoor environment unless the particular use has been checked by a competent person. In particular, the use of indoor load placement devices should not be used outdoors as load supporting devices.

After the structure has been commissioned, it is the responsibility of the User to satisfy himself that all reasonable steps have been taken to ensure the safety of the personnel who are erecting, operating and dismantling the system.

All works shall be carried out in accordance with the Health and Safety Regulations which are in force in the country or region where the roof structure is being used, and be structured and planned in such a way as to reduce risks of injury to an acceptable minimum. The use of risk assessments and method statements is recommended in undertaking planning and organisation of work.

This may involve forbidding 'climbing' access in favour of access equipment – self-propelled or scaffolding or other measures.

Certain jobs such as rigging the hoists and lifting the towers require special training and experience. Some risks can be controlled by assigning only such personnel to these tasks.

The correct use of properly designed and installed fall protection equipment may be necessary to prevent injury from a fall. Wearing of hard hats, safety boots and gloves should be considered necessary during certain parts of erection and dismantling of the structure.

As the industry has had a tendency to be somewhat cavalier in the past regarding safety issues, we should expect that the authorities will turn their attention to the entertainment industry in the not too distant future and introduce far reaching legislation. This is a real possibility in the UK where the Health and Safety Executive are examining a number of accidents which, in my view, were generally avoidable if a number of simple rules had been followed.

The construction industry has a very poor record of safety in the UK and throughout the world. The Health and Safety Executive introduced the Construction (Design and Management) Regulations in the UK a number of years ago and are now starting to enforce them vigorously. I understand that at present there are significant number of company directors in prison in the UK for breaches of these regulations - a salutary thought for many, I'm sure. Copies of these regulations can be obtained from the Health and Safety Executive.

If you are ever in doubt, ask!

Lighting designers, promoters and bands often require everything to be bigger and better than last time and often do not consider fully the structural implications of their requirements. They assume that because it worked last time, it will be OK this time.

Working at height

Safe working at height is becoming a huge issue for the entertainment industry. In fact it always has been an issue, but it has been brought under closer scrutiny in recent times. Statutory authorities are now turning their attention to the enforcement of the prohibition of free climbing in the construction industry in the UK, and this will inevitably lead to a review of best practice in other industries.

Some users tried to address the issue some time ago by applying fall arrest systems used in other industries to truss grids, lighting trusses and the like. However, in general, they failed to consider the impact of attaching such systems to the truss itself. They were, it could be argued, making the best of a bad job.

'Guaranteed for life?' which was published by ESTA's *Protocol* in Spring 1999 and in ABTT's *Update* shortly afterwards, discussed the issue of attaching fall arrest systems to trusses in some depth.

It is worth noting that both the American Standard, ANSI E1.2 'Design, Manufacture and use of Aluminum Trusses and Towers' and the

British Standard BS 7906 Part 2 Code of Practice for the Use of Aluminium and Steel Trusses and Towers require the user to determine all the loads on a truss, including those from fall arrest systems. The standards also state that the user shall consider the loads from fall arrest systems when determining if a truss is adequate.

'On your head be it?' was published by ABTT *Update* and ESTA's *Protocol* in September and October 2000 respectively. It was written to make people aware of the publication of the British and American standards.

Whilst the installation of vertical fall arrest systems by some building owners should be applauded, one should appreciate that they are responding to their responsibilities under law. This is something that has been sadly lacking by many in the entertainment industry for a number of years. One may argue that they should also be responsible for providing a safe 'mother grid' structure for use by touring shows and the like.

The forces on structures are more complex for horizontal (than vertical) fall arrest systems and cannot be ignored. They must be considered in detail and in conjunction with the structure or truss grid to which they are attached. One simply cannot design a fall arrest system in isolation. For example, you cannot only consider the capacity of a truss grid when checking the load plot for a particular show – the anchorages also have to be considered. The two go hand-in-hand.

One can argue that it is foolhardy to design a system to save life without considering the whole picture. When an engineer designs a building he starts at the roof and follows the loads all the way down to the foundations and then considers how the soil supports the foundation. This is a simple analogy, but one that is very relevant when considering the loads on a truss grid and then following them back to the anchorages and beyond.

If a fall arrest system is to be used in conjunction with a truss grid, then clearly the user should collaborate with the truss manufacturers or their technical advisers.

Sometimes it is not possible for engineers to provide simple rules that can be followed easily. The problem often contains too many variables. However, I would have thought that a yardstick could be provided by the companies advocating the use of a horizontal fall arrest system based on a catenary wire with a truss grid. Clearly, it would be necessary to down-rate the load-carrying capacity of the truss when it also carries a fall arrest system. A fall arrest system generally imposes an axial force in the chords, and this reduces the allowable bending moment in the truss for a given span. The allowable load can therefore be determined for that span. Each span is considered in turn and the allowable load against span graph can be plotted.

"If trusses are not strong enough..., then manufacturers must build them stronger," I heard from one quarter. The manufacturer generally has no control over the location or which fall arrest system will be used in conjunction with the truss he has fabricated. The loads imposed on the truss depend heavily on how shock absorbers are used and the distance between the supports to the fall arrest system. Many of the trusses within the grid may not be fitted with such a system.

The manufacturer trades in an ever-increasingly competitive market. Publishing allowable load data that includes a provision for a fall arrest system, whether it is provided or not, may not be helpful for the user as the strength of many of the trusses would be in excess of what is actually required. This would not be cost effective for the rental company or user.

We have now identified that we are trying to grapple with a very complex and emotive issue. But what can or has been done about it?

I am pleased to say that Total Fabrications Limited in the UK, has risen to the challenge. They understood that the use of conventional industrial fall-arrest equipment with existing truss systems does not necessarily provide a convenient, safe means for fall-arrest and rescue. They understood that there is an increased professionalism within the industry, with a greater awareness of good working practices and desire to comply with the spirit and letter of the law. They understood that advances in technology and performance requirements place new demands on equipment and personnel. They are not encouraging people to climb on trusses, but recognise that when it really is the only way to get the work done, a method of access is required that would be considered as a 'designed' safe working practice.

Development started in December 1999, and has followed a planned programme from concept generation and planning to implementation of production processes and procedures, including product definition and specification, concept feasibility and development, design, engineering analysis and testing, review of standards, legislation and approvals, detail design, prototyping and finally launch at PLASA 2000 where T2 won the Award for Product Excellence in the Stage Engineering Category.

T2 is a structural system with integral protection for personnel against falls from a height and addresses the various points that have been made previously regarding the use of proprietary fall arrest systems with trusses and truss grids. The key components include the truss, twin shock absorbing lanyards with mobile anchor points, fittings for hanging equipment, rigging hardware for installation and operation and finally accessories for utility and effect.

An integral part of the T2 system is the training which forms part of the package. Working at height is hazardous and T2 cannot be seen as doing anything to affect the severity of this hazard. Competent application and use of appropriate equipment can reduce the risks. This can only be sensibly achieved through aptitude, experience and training.

The T2 truss is a very different design from 'standard' trusses used in the entertainment industry. The differences are quite deliberate - some have arisen from necessity, whilst others are the result of questioning and then rejecting preconceived ideas of the form which trusses 'should' have. For example, the chords of a truss should always be 2" diameter round or scaffold tube so that hook clamps and scaffold couplers can be used. Yet current best practice is not to use hook clamps as they damage the tube, scaffold couplers are 'rated', but have no reference to how tight they should be and in which direction the load can be applied. We all know how treacherous wet or damp round tubes can be underfoot.

The chords of the truss are constructed from a custom designed extrusion, not round tube. The square profile has safety benefits; it is more comfortable to walk along reducing operator fatigue; and its ribbed surface makes the user more foot-sure and facilitates the inspection of the chords for excessive abrasion.

A 'T' channel is integrated into the extrusion on all four chords and the dedicated twin shock absorbing lanyard assemblies fix directly to this channel, providing a mobile but direct anchor point. The mobile anchor point requires a number of distinct actions to either engage or disengage from the 'T' channel and full connection cannot be mistaken. Two anchor points are required to traverse any obstructions along the 'T' channel. By applying the load associated with an arrested fall directly to a chord, the issue of large forces in chords and / or anchorages from catenary wires is bypassed. The extrusion was used on all four chords so that the fall arrest system could be used above or below the truss.

Now that the 'T' channel was to be used on all chords, a method was neatly established for all attachment needs - personnel security, lighting, video and audio - dispensing with the need for hook clamps or scaffold couplers. The 'T' clamp was developed and various styles and sizes are contemplated to carry a range of maximum safe working loads. The connectors also feature this channel. A fixing can now be made at any location along a run of truss instead of being hindered by the form of the connectors, bracing (diagonals) and the like where some 30% of a 'standard' truss cannot be used.

The connectors are made from very high grade aluminium alloy and their strength is consistent with that of the chord, so ensuring maximum efficiency and therefore load carrying capacity of the truss. The alloy used in the connectors cannot be welded and hence they are pinned to the chords. The thickness of the extrusion at the bearing of these pins is proportional to the allowable load transfer. The thickness of the various parts of the chord are such as to provide full load transfer from chord to chord whilst keeping the weight of the completed truss to a minimum. The connector itself is a form of fork connector which are in widespread use in industry. However, they are genderless and hence the truss can be connected in a number of orientations.

It is widely accepted that significant loads should be applied at node points on trusses and most allowable load data provided by manufacturers highlight this point. The chord extrusion for T2 has been designed to resist loads associated with an arrested fall at any location, including between nodes. A by-product of this requirement is that significant loads can be applied anywhere along the chord, including those associated with supporting the truss.

The trussing web - its diagonal bracing - is also quite different from what has been seen before. By passing the web in 3D through the centre of the truss, sufficient bracing is provided to resist the loads from an arrested fall which could occur in any direction. This feature also reduces the amount of components, so keeping weight to a minimum, as well as making the traversing of the truss easier and less hazardous. The diameter and thickness of the diagonals and secondary members are optimised for structural performance whilst keeping weight to a minimum.

The type and means of rescue was another major issue tackled by the design team. Clearly, the safest way to rescue someone is to lower the grid after clearing the area below. If a system based on a catenary wire is used to arrest a fall from height, then the user must pay particular attention to the amount of travel required before the fall is arrested. This means that a clearance of 5 to 10 metres below the grid may be required. If the person is unconscious and is left 'dangling' in mid air for more than about 10 minutes, then he will probably die through constriction of some of the major arteries in his body by the harness. The rescuers now have to reach the person some distance above the ground in a limited time after the fall. T2 approaches the problem in a different way. The lanyard is relatively short and hence the distance of fall is limited and self-rescue would normally be expected. In the event of the person being unconscious, the rescuers can traverse the truss as normal and effect the rescue from just below the truss.

By starting with a blank piece of paper and rejecting many of the design 'constraints', the truss that forms part of the T2 system is highly efficient both structurally and volumetrically.

Developed and designed by in-house structural and mechanical engineers and safety experts from within the entertainment industry, the T2 system addresses many issues of safer working at height in a completely integrated fashion. With greater strength and improved practical performance compared with traditional products with added features to enable fall-arrest and rescue, the T2 truss was described by one observer as a 'quantum leap forward'.

Example of T2 truss system.

T2 Truss fall arrest system in operation

16 THE FUTURE

So how far can we go? What are the limitations? How far can we push the envelope?

This is a difficult question to answer.

The Budweiser tower for the Atlanta Olympic Games was about 80 feet high – the equivalent to an eight storey building.

The loudspeaker support towers for the 'BZs' in Japan were nearly 25 metres high and each carried eight tonnes of loudspeakers. They were originally designed for use indoors but after a few more calculations I managed to accept they could be used outdoors under certain conditions.

100 foot long catwalks were designed and fabricated for use over the audience at the Wet Wet Wet tour in the early 1990s. This was the first time in

Budweiser Tower at the Atlanta Olympics

BZs towers at the Tokyo Dome, Tokyo

Nike Pavillion at the Atlanta Olympics, 1996

the industry to my knowledge, that large moving loads have been suspended directly over an audience.

The Nike Pavilion at the Atlanta Olympic Games in 1996 was a huge undertaking and comprised a 'butterfly' structure with 'wings' each measuring over 100 feet by 60 feet.

The stage sets produced for groups such as Pink Floyd, the Rolling Stones and U2 are much-admired as examples of what the entertainment industry can achieve. These are at the leading edge of the touring market and many other much smaller shows should also receive considerable accolades.

So we can see that many things have been attempted with a degree of success. But what else can be done? The size and weight of aluminium structures which are required to support ever increasing loads and spans are starting to become unmanageable and are more difficult to handle manually. Hence, steel structures have been adopted by some companies to meet their needs. These are often considerably cheaper than the conventional aluminium structures which are so widespread in the industry.

Nike Pavillion at the Atlanta Olympics, 1996

However, standard and bespoke aluminium trusses and towers remain the 'work horses' of the industry and will probably remain so for a considerable time to come as rental and production companies have invested heavily in such equipment in the past.

Entertainment technology has made some large strides in the past 25 years. Particular landmarks which spring to mind include the introduction of the first moving light, advances in pyrotechnics and multiple hoist control.

Aluminium trusses have been used in various styles and forms to meet a range of different applications. Generic trusses such as 20.5" and 12" square box truss are offered by a selection of manufacturers and can now be seen at most trade shows in a variety of countries around the world.

Unlike other parts of the entertainment world, truss technology has changed very little since it all began – trusses are a little wider, a little deeper, perhaps with double or single fork ends or even turnbuckles instead of end plates which are connected with nuts and bolts, or perhaps folding to reduce storage and transportation costs. No really significant, fundamental changes or approaches have been seen in recent years, perhaps with the exception of T2 which integrated a fall arrest system into truss design and was launched at PLASA in 2001 by Total Fabrications and the OMNI connector by Total Structures which was adapted and used in the 'new wave' truss system discussed below.

"The introduction of carbon fibre into the truss market is both innovative and very appropriate – it is about time we had a new look" was just one of the many comments received at the Total Structures booth at LDI 2002 in Las Vegas.

The following describes the development of the "new wave" product range and discusses the philosophy and the problems which were encountered along the way. The main discussion revolves around the carbon fibre variant known as c-wave, but mention is also made of the aluminium and Plexiglas variants known as a-wave and p-wave respectively.

Carbon fibre and high strength epoxy adhesives have been part of other technologically advanced industries for some time. The automotive industry is a case in point – the use of carbon fibre is widespread in Formula 1 and Lotus Cars use epoxy adhesives to bond the aluminium chassis elements together. Carbon fibre "look alike" dashboards are frequently seen in the production cars which are on the roads today.

Having appreciated that this technology exists, the team at Total Structures linked up with an OEM composite manufacturer and started to develop a structural, aesthetically pleasing, system with a range of finishes for a variety of markets, one of which being entertainment.

The obvious form would be to use the same pattern of chords and diagonals as used in regular aluminium trusses or much of the built environment in which we live. This form, however, does not lend itself to high strength connections without an industrial look which could be likened to bonded plastic plumbing products.

A less obvious solution would be to form the diagonals and end frames from a plate. Holes would be provided for the chords to pass through and other perforations are provided to reduce the weight of the plate. This is a useful feature as the chords will be protected from abrasion if the truss were to be dragged along the floor (which is never to be recommended). The chords would then be bonded using a high strength epoxy adhesive. However, the plates would need to be accurate to ensure the chord centres were maintained for ease of connection to the next truss and to be attractive. Water jet cutting was considered and the early prototypes used this form of plate. However, the cost of cutting such plates was high and therefore an alternative had to be found.

As all the plates had the same profile, an extrusion was clearly the solution and this could be cut at an angle to form the diagonal plates or perpendicular to form the end plates. A mill was sourced and discussions took place on the level of tolerance that could be achieved, with the chord centres and the diameter of the hole for the chords being the critical dimensions of the final aluminium extrusion.

Clearly, the hole diameter for the chords has to be carefully considered. Firstly, the diameter needs to be sufficient to allow the easy passage of the chords during assembly so that the chords are not scratched. Secondly, and conversely, the holes for the chords need to be a diameter which permits the correct thickness of the adhesive. So a compromise has to be found to facilitate assembly but enable a full strength connection to be achieved. The adhesive, therefore, has to exhibit a range of characteristics, such as a thicker bond line, but also with a sufficient period of time between application and

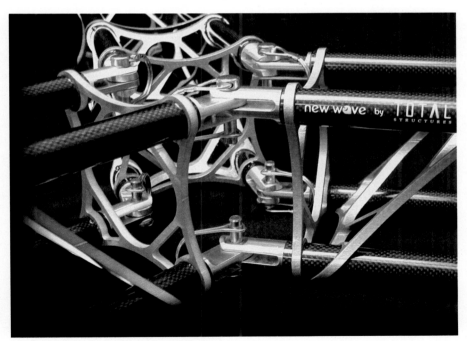

Six inch square section 'new wave' truss.

initial set (again for ease of assembly), a clear or non-obtrusive colour for aesthetic reasons, and high strength in both normal and high temperature environments.

This last requirement warranted a certain amount of research. What transpired is that the heat resistance of epoxy resin adhesives is linked to the cure temperature. The cured epoxy adhesive will soften when subjected to a temperature well above the cure temperature. It would be useful at this point to consider what actually happens to aluminium trusses at elevated temperatures. This is clearly described by the following graph which shows the relationship between temperature and strength of 6061-T6 aluminium, the alloy commonly used in entertainment industry in the United States.

A bi-product of the use of an extrusion to form the diagonals and the end plates is that it can be utilized to provide branding opportunities for the truss.

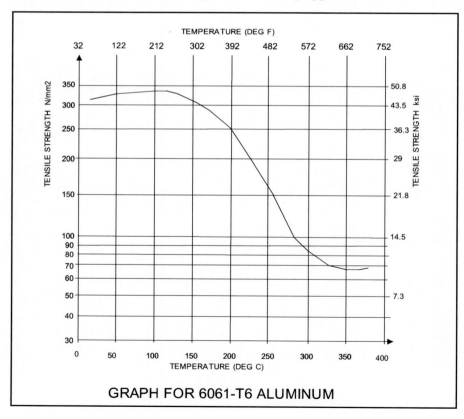

GRAPH FOR 6061-T6 ALUMINUM

Corporate logos can easily be cut from the extrusion using a process known as "edm" – electrical discharge machine. A thin wire is electrically charged and is used to cut the material underwater. This form is cutting is non abrasive and is highly accurate.

Another, less expensive, branding opportunity has only recently become available. The technology to print onto carbon fibre has been developed and has now become commercially available. The final "wrap" of the carbon fibre tube is the printed sheet and so now virtually any form of artwork can be applied to the chords, be it pattern, photographic images, corporate logos and messages, or whatever. It makes a very exciting proposition for marketing personnel for use in trade show booths, exhibitions, retail, corporate installations and the like.

Alternatively, the final "wrap" can be replaced with ribbons of "Kevlar" which can be died in a range of colours to form a variety of effects. This finish is particularly vibrant when bathed in light. The diagonal and end plates can be anodized to match the chord finishes, with stunning effect, or they can be a variety of colours – a look that has never been seen before in regular trussing in the entertainment industry.

Two major concerns about the use of carbon fibre in trussing were impact damage and the ability to hang loads without damage to the chords. Extensive impact damage tests were carried out on the raw tubes. These included a given (significant) mass falling a set distance onto the tube in both single and multiple actions. The potential and kinetic energy of the impact could then be determined. The conclusion was that multiple blows on one location resulted

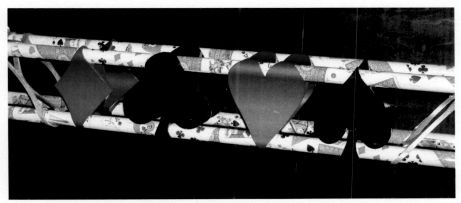

Printed sheet final 'wrap' and 'edm' cut shapes on new wave truss.

in slight delamination of the outer fibres. Whilst this is undesirable, it would not cause failure of the truss as the connector has a lower tensile and compression strength than the chord itself. It should be appreciated that this level of impact could not have been sustained by aluminium tubing of a similar diameter and wall thickness. The truss is lightweight and therefore there would be a small amount of inertia and momentum if it fell against a relatively sharp object but it was found that it simply bounced off without damage.

The attachment of fixtures or other loads to truss has been the subject of much discussion in the past. As with aluminium trusses, the use of half couplers or other purpose made clamps are recommended, with the obvious exception of C clamps or other devices which impose concentrated point loads on the wall of the chord.

An incredibly decorative version of the 'new wave' series is under development and was also shown at the 2002 LDI Show. While the same patented construction techniques are used, it is made entirely from Plexiglas. Known as p-wave, it really comes into its own when lit. The edges of the Plexi capture the light and the truss positively glows with the color it is bathed in. The illustrations clearly show the alluring potential of p-wave to become not just the structure for lighting support but part of the light show itself.

The a-wave is the grandfather of the new wave series in that it uses traditional aluminum chords with the extruded 'plate' technology. Within the range, it is Pound for Pound, the most efficient variant whilst retaining the unique good looks of the form.

The a-wave offers several unique faces to the world of modular truss in addition to the more typical polished 'silver' and powder coated finishes. The aluminum can be anodized in a range of colors, and as the assembly is 'bonded', the chords can be colored in complementary colors to the 'plates'. This can be further enhanced by anodizing the extrusion prior to cutting, which has the effect of highlighting the faces of the plates in silver.

A range of accessories have been developed for use with the truss. The detachable rigging point is designed to attach in between any pair of diagonals and centrally to the width of the truss. It is quick to install and has a load capacity of 350 kg (750 lbs). The rigging point is also invertible and becomes an ideal fixture hanger (or both). 25.4 mm (1") half couplers are also available to hang equipment from the chords without damaging the tube. Special adaptors allow the hanging of most moving lights and heavier equipment.

The spreader bar allows the setting of angles (where the structure is not

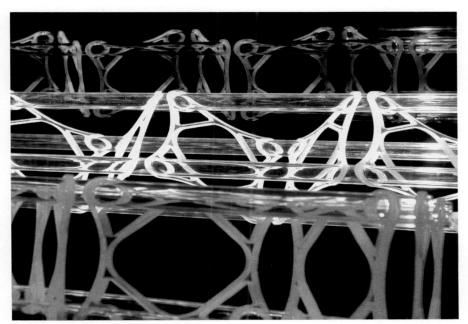

P-wave Plexiglass truss.

already rigid) and also provides an aesthetic finish to open corners. Modular in nature, the length can be adjusted by using different lengths of tube.

OMNI-p is a versatile variation of the same connector used in the truss. OMNI-p is used in the spreaders, bases and also to create perpendicular connections in the third dimension, for example to create a 90 degree corner with a leg.

The 'new wave' truss by Total Structures uses a variant of the award winning OMNI connector, so that most two- and three-dimensional structures can be assembled without the need for complex (and therefore expensive) fixed corner blocks. The lengths of the tangs of the unisex fork ends are set so that angles of 45 degrees can be achieved between adjacent truss modules. Articulation of joints is also easily achieved to form a multitude of two- and three-dimensional forms.

Needless to say, a number of aspects of the new wave system are the subject of world-wide intellectual property and patent protection.

All in all, new wave is a radical departure from regular aluminium truss which has become so widely used and ultimately somewhat 'tired'. It provides much greater flexibility and branding opportunities for the client. The aesthetic qualities of new wave have never been seen before – not only the chords, but also within the structure itself. The range of colour and texture, combined with branding opportunities, is limitless.

This is just one exciting and innovative development. There will, no doubt, be many others in the years to come as the entertainment industry tries to find solutions to both old and new problems. The application of sound structural engineering principles, an increased awareness of safety matters, a better appreciation by users of structural issues and more varied and adventurous rigging techniques mean that we can look forward to achieving even more impressive and expressive structures in the entertainment industry.

However, the industry must continue along the path of increased professionalism, more accountability and the acknowledgement of individual and corporate responsibility.

Photo courtesy of Shiki.

Principal Manufacturers of Structural Trussing Systems

James Thomas Engineering Inc
10603 Lexington Drive, Knoxville, Tennessee 37932 USA
Tel +1 423 671 2885, Fax +1 423 671 2886
www.jamesthomas.com

James Thomas Engineering Ltd
Navigation Complex, Navigation Road, Diglis Trading Estate,
Worcester WR5 3DE, UK
Tel +44 1906 363600, Fax +44 1906 363601
www.jamesthomas.com

Litestructures (GB) Ltd
Unit 55, Ludgate Crescent, Langthwaite
Grange Industrial Estate, South Kirkby, Wakefield,
West Yorkshire WF9 3NR, UK
Tel +44 1977 659800, Fax +44 1977 659801
www.litestructures.co.uk

Prolyte Products Group
Industriepark 9, NL 9351 PA Leek, The Netherlands
Tel +31 594 851515, Fax +31 594 851516
www.prolyte.com

Tomcat UK Ltd
Unit 2, Skiddaw Road, Croft Industrial Estate,
Bromborough, Wirral CH62 3RB, UK
Tel +44 151 482 3100
Fax +44 151 482 3111
www.tomcatglobal.com

Tomcat USA Inc
2160 Commerce, Midland, Texas 79703, USA
Tel +1 915 694 7070, Fax +1 915 689 3805
www.tomcatglobal.com

Total Fabrications Limited
Units 3-6 Kingston Industrial Estate
81-86 Glover Street, Birmingham B9 4EN, West Midlands, UK
Tel +44 121 772 5234, Fax +44 121 772 5231
www.totalfabs.com

Total Structures Inc
1696 Walter Street, Ventura, California 93003, USA
Tel +1 805 676 3322, Fax +1 805 676 1616
www.totalstructures.com

GLOSSARY

ABTT
Association of British Theatre Technicians

ANSI
American National Standards Institute

ASCE
American Society of Civil Engineers

Abrasion
Loss of material due to wear

Allowable load
Maximum static equivalent load imposed on truss / tower in addition to the self-weight

Ancillary
Supplementary

BRE
Building Research Establishment

BSI
British Standards Institute

Bent member, truss or tower
Permanent inelastic deviation from the intended centre line

Bolted connection
A connection of two truss modules using bolts

Buckling
Permanent lateral displacement of a strut (element of a truss module) from the original centreline under axial load, usually sudden

Camber
Intended vertical deviation of a truss, usually radiused

Centre Point Load (C.P.L.)
A load that is applied to the centre of the truss

Chord
Element of the truss or tower module that carry axial forces associated with flexure or axial loading

Components
Parts of a whole

Connecting plates
Plates welded to the ends frames of a truss or tower module that are used to connect adjacent modules together

Consumables
Items that require regular replacement with use

Corner
Usually a cube, a module with connections on a number of faces to provide a junction between a number of trusses

Crack
A crevice type discontinuity in the material

Damage
Condition that adversely affects the intended use of truss module (usually load carrying capacity)

Dent
Local deformation resulting in measurable change in cross section of member or element

Design strength
Capacity of the elements of the structure to withstand normal design loading

Diagonal
Elements of the truss or tower module that are at an angle to the main chords

Drift test / flare test
A standard test undertaken on aluminium tubing to check structural integrity of the tube walls, in particular, the test highlights splits in the tube which can occur in the extrusion process

Dye penetrant testing
A standard non destructive test that highlights cracks in welds but does not affect the integrity of the weld or the parent metal

Dynamic loading
A load which moves or vibrates

ESTA
Entertainment and Services Technology Association, USA

End plate
A plate on end of a truss module allowing connection to adjacent truss module(s)

HSE
Health and Safety Executive

Incident
Occurrence where damage to one or more truss module is or may be sustained

IStructE
Institution of Structural Engineers

KPH
Kilometres per hour

Lacing member
Secondary members between the chords

Lateral torsional buckling
The buckling of a truss or tower accompanied by a combination of lateral displacement and twisting

Lateral restraint
Restraint that limits lateral movement of the compression chords of the truss or tower

Limit state
Condition beyond which a structure is unfit for its intended use

LRFD
Load Resistance Factor Design

Manufacturer
Person or company who fabricates truss / tower modules or systems

Module
Singular framed structure that is built up entirely from tension and compression members, arranged in panels so as to be stable under load

Multiple use
truss or tower system assembly designed specifically for use at one or more locations and erected on more than one occasion

MPH
Miles per hour

Node point
Junction of one or more lacing members with a chord (see also panel point)

ND-T
Non-destructive testing

OSHA
Occupational Safety and Health Administration

Panel point
Junction of one or more lacing members with a chord (see also node point)

Pinned connection:
end tube connection that uses a removable pin to effect a connection between truss modules

PLASA
Professional Light and Sound Association, UK

Qualified person
A person who, by possession of a recognised degree or certificate of professional standing, or who by extensive knowledge, training, and experience, has successfully demonstrated the ability to solve problems relating to the subject matter and work

Quarter point load (Q.P.L.)
A load that is applied at a distance of a quarter, half and three quarters of the span from one end of the truss

Regular service
Normal repetitive use

Repetitive use
Truss or tower modules assembled and dismantled an multiple occasions

Resonance
The phenomenon resulting from synchronism between a pronounced periodicity in the loading process and a natural vibration frequency of the structure and lead to gross magnification of response

Serviceability limit states
Those limit states that when exceeded can lead to the structure being unfit for its intended use, even though the structure has not collapsed

Single use
Truss or tower system assembly designed specifically for one location, erected once and left in place

Shall
indicates that the rule is mandatory and must be followed

Should
Indicates that the rule is a recommendation, the advisability of which depends on the facts and conditions in each situation

Skin
A material cover to a truss structure (usually on a roof system)

Sleeve
Usually a cube, a module with connections on a number of faces to provide a junction between a number of trusses, but with internal wheels to allow a tower to pass through. Usually used with a ground support system or roof structure

Slenderness ratio
The effective length divided by the radius of gyration.

Span
The distance between support points

Static load
A load which is not moving

Sweep
Intended lateral deviation of a truss, usually radiused

Temporary
Not permanent. Reference shall be made to local building codes for relevant definitions

Third point load (T.P.L.)
A load that is applied at a distance of a third of the span from each end of the truss

Tower
One or more modules assembled vertically to carry primarily axial load usually square or triangular

Truss
One or more modules assembled to carry load over a distance, generally horizontal, primarily in flexure

UBC
Uniform Building Code, USA

User
Person or company who assembles or uses truss or tower modules or systems

Uniformly distributed load (U.D.L.)

A load that is evenly spread over the length of the truss (usually as a discreet loads at each node or panel point)

CONVERSION FACTORS

Quantity	From Inch-Pound Units	To Metric Units	Multiply by
Mass	lb kip (1000 lb)	kg metric ton (1000 kg)	0.453 592 0.453 592
Mass / unit length	plf	kg/m	1.488 16
Mass / unit area	psf	kg/m2	4.882 43
Mass density	pcf	kg/m3	16.018 5
Force	lbkip	N kN	4.448 22 4.448 22
Force / unit length	plf klf	N/m kN/m	14.953 9 14.953 9
Pressure, stress, modulus of elasticity	psf ksf psi ksi	Pa (N/m2) kPa (kN/m2) kPa (kN/m2) MPa (N/mm2)	47.880 3 47.880 3 6.894 76 6.894 76
Bending moment, torque, moment of force	ft-lb ft-kip	N.m kN.m	1.355 82 1.355 82
Moment of mass	lb.ft	kg.m	0.138 255
Moment of inertia	in4	mm4	416.231
Section modulus	in3	mm3	16 387.064
Length	mile yard foot foot inch	km m m mm mm	1.609 344 0.914 4 0.304 8 304.8 25.4
Area	square yard square foot square inch	m2 m2 mm2	0.836 127 0.092 903 645.16
Volume	cubic yard cubic foot cubic foot gallon (US liquid) cubic inch cubic inch	m3 m3 L (1000 cm3) L (1000cm3) cm3 mm3	0.764 555 0.836 127 28.316 85 3.785 41 16.387 064 16 387.064
Speed	miles per hour	m/s	0.447 04

BIBLIOGRAPHY & FURTHER READING

Bibliography

BS 8118 The Structural Use of Aluminium
British Standards Institute 1992

BS 6399 Design Loads for Buildings
British Standards Institute Various

ANSI E1.2 Design, Manufacture and Use of Modular Aluminium Trusses and Towers
American National Standards Institute 2000

ASCE 7 Design Loads for Structures During Construction
American Society for Civil Engineers

ASCE 37 Minimum Design Loads for Buildings and Other Structures
American Society for Civil Engineers

Uniform Building Code – Volume 2 Structural Engineering Design Provisions
International Conference of Building Officials

Factors of Safety in Aluminum Structures
Peter Hind and David M Campbell
Protocol Magazine, Journal of ESTA Summer 1997

Loads, What Loads?
Peter Hind
Protocol Magazine, Journal of ESTA Spring 1998

Gone With The Wind?
Peter Hind
Protocol Magazine, Journal of ESTA Autumn 1998

Guaranteed for life?
Peter Hind
Protocol Magazine, Journal of ESTA Spring 1999

Built on firm foundations?
Peter Hind
Protocol Magazine, Journal of ESTA Autumn 1999

On your head be it?
Peter Hind
Protocol Magazine, Journal of ESTA Autumn 2000

new wave – The Introduction of Carbon Fibre Truss
Peter Hind
Entertainment Technology November 2002

Painted Trusses – All dressed up and nowhere to go?
Peter Hind
Protocol Magazine, Journal of ESTA Spring 2003

Outdoor Stages – Keep your feet on the ground
Peter Hind
Protocol Magazine, Journal of ESTA Summer 2003

Temporary Demountable Structures - Second Edition
Institution of Structural Engineers, UK March 1999

BRE Digest 284
Building Research Establishment, UK 1986

BRE Digest 390
Building Research Establishment, UK January 1994

The Properties of Aluminium and it's Alloys
Aluminium Federation Ltd August 1993

Further Reading

Structures or why things don't fall down
Professor JE Gordon
Da Capo Press, Inc, New York, USA

The New Science of Strong Materials or why you don't fall through the floor
Professor JE Gordon
Penguin Books Ltd, London, UK

An Introduction to Rigging in the Entertainment Industry
Chris Higgs
Entertainment Technology Press

Rigging for Entertainment: Regulations and Practice
Chris Higgs
Entertainment Technology Press

Specifications for Aluminum Structures
The Aluminum Association
Aluminum Association, Inc, Washington, USA

Safe Use of Work Equipment
Provision and Use of Work Equipment Regulations 1998
Health and Safety Commission, UK

Safe Use of Lifting Equipment
Lifting Operations and Lifting Equipment Regulations 1998
Health and Safety Commission, UK

Factors Affecting the Load Carrying Capacity of Ground Anchors Used to Support Temporary Structures
ME/98/02 February 1998
Health and Safety Laboratory, UK

Temporary Demountable Structures - Second Edition
March 1999
Institution of Structural Engineers, UK

The Event Safety Guide - Guidance to Health, Safety and Welfare at Music and Similar Events
HSG195
Health and Safety Commission

BS 7905 Lifting Equipment for Performance, Broadcast and Similar Applications, Part 2 Specification for the Design and Manufacture of Aluminium and Steel Trusses and Towers
British Standards Institute

BS 7906 Lifting Equipment for Performance, Broadcast and Similar Applications, Part 2 Code of Practice for the Use of Aluminium and Steel Trusses and Towers
British Standards Institute

ANSI E1.2 Design, Manufacture and Use of Modular Aluminium Trusses and Towers
American National Standards Institute

INDEX

ENTERTAINMENT TECHNOLOGY PRESS

FREE SUBSCRIPTION SERVICE

Keeping Up To Date with

Aluminium Structures in the Entertainment Industry

Entertainment Technology Press titles are continually up-dated, and all changes and additions are listed in date order in the relevant dedicated area of the publisher's website. Simply go to the front page of www.etnow.com and click on the BOOKS button. From there you can locate the title and be connected through to the latest information and services related to the publication, including the tender specification examples in this book available for download.

The author of Aluminium Structures in the Entertainment Industry welcomes comments and suggestions about this book and can be contacted by email at peterh@totalstructures.com